TEXAS
DISASTERS

DISASTERS SERIES

TEXAS
DISASTERS

TRUE STORIES OF
TRAGEDY AND SURVIVAL

Mike Cox

INSIDERS' GUIDE®

GUILFORD, CONNECTICUT
AN IMPRINT OF THE GLOBE PEQUOT PRESS

INSIDERS'GUIDE®

Text design by Pettistudio LLC, www.pettistudio.com
Map by M. A. Dubé © Morris Book Publishing, LLC

Library of Congress Cataloging-in-Publication Data
Cox, Mike, 1948–
  Texas disasters : true stories of tragedy and survival / Mike Cox. — 1st ed.
     p. cm. — (Disasters series)
  Includes bibliographical references.
  ISBN-13: 978-0-7627-3675-1
  ISBN-10: 0-7627-3675-5
  1. Disasters—Texas—History—Anecdotes. 2. Texas—History, Local—
Anecdotes. I. Title. II. Series.
  F386.6.C69 2006
  976.4—dc22

                                                        2006011671

Manufactured in the United States of America
First Edition/First Printing

Contents

Preface

One piece of conventional wisdom about the writing business is that an author should always stick to what he knows. If that truly makes a difference, I have seen more than my share of disasters over the years.

During a nearly twenty-year career as a reporter in Texas, I covered numerous fires, traffic accidents, plane crashes, floods, hurricanes, tornadoes, and assorted other mass-casualty situations. Later, during the fifteen years I spent as spokesman for the Texas Department of Public Safety, I stood on the other side of the yellow crime-scene tape to give members of the news media information on many more tragedies.

But visiting a disaster scene after the fact is very different from being a disaster survivor.

I didn't view myself as a survivor of the deadly May 11, 1970, Lubbock tornado at first, but I later learned that the twister first dropped from the clouds near the intersection of Sixty-sixth and University Streets in that South Plains city, only a few blocks from the duplex where I lived.

Hearing on the radio that a tornado had been reported, I had followed what then was a recommended safety procedure: I opened all the windows. Though the theory has long since been disproved, the thinking back then was that open windows kept a house from exploding due to the sudden drop in barometric pressure associated with a tornado. In truth, nothing can save a house hit by a large twister.

I never actually saw the tornado because it was nighttime. But I heard its roar. It didn't sound like the freight train so many tornado survivors describe, but the giant twister did play tricks with the air pressure, causing my duplex's curtains to suck in and out of the windows I had opened.

The thunderstorm that spawned the tornado struck on a Monday night, which happened to be the last night of my regular days off at the *Avalanche-Journal,* the city's newspaper. As soon as I realized the severity of the situation, I knew my colleagues would need all the help they could get. Maneuvering around downed power lines and other debris cluttering the streets, I drove to the newspaper and worked for most of the rest of the night.

The next morning, with the city's water service disrupted, I drank my first—and I hope last—toilet-tank–water coffee. (Water from the tank is potable. Just don't get it mixed up.) For me, the Lubbock tornado only meant long hours at work and some degree of inconvenience, as in being without electricity and water for a while. Unlike so many others, I had not been hurt or lost my home. And twenty-six people lost their lives that night. Still, it was a close call that left me with both a healthy appreciation of what a tornado can do and a much better understanding of what it is like to go through a disaster.

Despite the fact that I experienced it firsthand, I didn't include the Lubbock tornado in this book because Texas has seen much worse. Even so, living through it gave me a good feel for what the aftermath of disaster is like.

After writing the manuscript for this book, I became involved in the dual disasters of Hurricanes Katrina and Rita in the summer of 2005. As communications manager for the Texas Department of Transportation, I helped coordinate the release of public information on TxDOT's role in assisting the hundreds of thousands of evacuees who streamed into Texas in cars, trucks, and buses from the stricken state of Louisiana in late August.

Thousands of people wait to enter the Disaster Recovery Center, or DRC, as it reopens after Hurricane Rita. Hundreds of FEMA workers were inside prepared to help. PHOTO BY ED EDAHL/FEMA

When the enormity of the disaster in and around New Orleans became apparent, my wife Linda and daughter Hallie volunteered their assistance in helping evacuees as busloads of them arrived to stay in a large emergency shelter set up at the Austin Convention Center. Our family, as did thousands of others in Texas, donated clothing and other items as well.

For Texas, the difficulties in coping with the in-migration from Louisiana because of Katrina proved only a dress rehearsal for Hurricane Rita, a storm which for a time took dead aim on the densely populated Houston-Galveston area.

Shortly after 6 A.M. on September 22, 2005, I got a call at home from Scott Alley, TxDOT's emergency management coordinator. "The governor has ordered us to contraflow Inter-state 45 north from Houston," he said. "We need you to get the word out to the public right now."

"Contraflow" is engineer talk for making major highways temporarily one-way, something never before done in Texas. As soon as I got off the phone with Alley, I called an 800-number for the Associated Press's Dallas bureau with the first official word of the momentous impending traffic develop-ment, the beginning of a very long couple of days for several million people, many of the employees of TxDOT included.

The undertaking proved to be the largest evacuation in the history of the world, the relocation of more than two million people in forty-eight hours. Texas will face the same prospect again during any given hurricane season.

Texans always pitch in and help each other after a tragedy, as I hope this book demonstrates. Of course, it doesn't take a disaster to get help from people. In researching this book, I got a lot of help from a wide range of "relief workers" who cheer-fully came to my assistance in putting together these stories.

Those who helped in researching or collecting images for this book include Carolyn Anderson and Tooter Smith of Rock-springs's *Mohair Weekly;* Chris David, manager of the Rock-springs Hotel, and his mother-in-law, Mildred Fleischer Williams; Gary McKee, then with the Texas Historical Commis-sion and one of Texas's leading experts on the state's maritime archaeology, and Steve Hatchcock, Padre Island history buff, both of whom helped with the Spanish shipwrecks story; old friend Larry BeSaw, a former reporter for the Wichita Falls *Times and Record News,* Texas Department of Transportation public information officer Adele Lewis, and former TxDOT PIO Dale Terry, who helped with the Wichita Falls tornado story;

longtime friend Richard Sims of Deer Park, who helped gather
information on the Gulf Hotel fire in Houston; TxDOT public
information officer Sabra Vaughn of Paris (Texas), a fellow state
worker who found the panoramic photo of Paris after the 1916
fire; Henry and Linda Wolff of Victoria, fellow authors and
Texas Folklore Society members, who helped with the stories of
the Indianola hurricanes and the Goliad tornado; TxDOT public information officer Glen Larum of Odessa and former
Sanderson resident Dee Mullins, who helped round up pictures
of the Sanderson flood; and Mary Lenz, public information officer for the state's Division of Emergency Management.

Friend and coworker Buddy Allison scanned several of the
images in this book and added to my education of things digital. Coworker Jeremy Boehm also helped with some scanning.

Also, Edward Meza, Director of the Laguna Madre
Museum in Port Isabel; Carlyn Hammons of the Texas Medical
Association Special Collections; Dean Johnstone of the Roseate
Spoonbill Gallery in Port Lavaca; Doris Freer from the Goliad
County Historical Commission and Museum; John Anderson
with the Photo Collection at the Texas State Library in Austin;
Bill Grigg of the New London School Explosion Museum; Joel
Draut of the Houston Municipal Research Collection at the
Houston Public Library; Betty Bustos of the Panhandle Plains
Museum in Canyon, Texas; Penny Clark of the Terrell Histori-
cal Library; the U.S. Coast Guard Photo Shop; and Blanca
Smith of the Special Collections Division, University of Texas
at Arlington.

I don't know anyone who could write a nonfiction book
without the help of librarians. Gayle Brown, Amarillo Public
Library; Judy Vickers, Paris Public Library; Suzanne Campbell
and Alexander S. Cano, Angelo State University West Texas

Collection; Frank Faulkner and his staff at the San Antonio Public Library's Texas Collection; and Barton Hill, Victoria Public Library, all were particularly helpful.

And special thanks to Anne Holliman, a photo editor for The Globe Pequot Press, who located many of the images and pulled them and others together for the book; Amy Paradysz, assistant managing editor, who took on this book project midway and managed it through production; and Joanna Beyer, the production coordinator who went the extra mile.

My mother, retired librarian Betty Wilke Cox, helped with the Galveston and Texas City chapters.

Finally, my wife Linda—as always—helped with research and with editing the first draft, locating illustrations, and reading the proofs.

Thanks to everyone. I hope that helping me with this book will prove to be as close to disaster as any of you ever gets.

Mike Cox
Austin, Texas

Introduction

Since its first known disaster—the wreck of three Spanish ships off the coast of South Padre Island in 1554—Texas has seen more than two score disasters each killing fourteen or more persons.

Weather has by far been the biggest killer in Texas, though man-made disasters have done their deadly share. The number-one killer in terms of body count has been hurricanes, but that is only because of the 1900 Galveston storm, which claimed anywhere from 6,000 to twice that many lives.

Historically, tornadoes have been the Texas weather event most likely to claim multiple victims. Nineteen times, twisters in the state have killed at a disastrous level, followed by seventeen killer hurricanes. While hurricanes are most common in September, May sees the highest number of tornadoes each year, followed by April. But one killer twister struck East Texas in January.

Third-most common among dangerous weather events are floods, which have resulted in multiple fatalities fourteen times in the state's recorded history. Though floods seldom result in mass casualties anymore, they still are the most prolific weather-related killer in Texas, claiming an average of fifteen lives a year, mostly at low-water crossings.

Mass casualties from other forms of severe weather are rarer. Only one nontornadic thunderstorm has left mass casualties in the state's history. Only two heat waves have killed in substantial numbers, and only one blizzard has had widespread effect.

As fierce as Texas weather has been and continues to be, thanks to improved forecasting, more accurate detection methods, and better warning systems, the incidence of storm-related fatalities has decreased greatly over the years. No tornado in Texas has killed more than forty-two people since 1953, no flood has claimed more than thirty-three lives since 1921, and no hurricane has killed more than thirty people since 1961.

(Striking the Texas coast on September 24, 2005, Hurricane Rita has been blamed for some 141 deaths, but only six of those could be directly related to the storm. The rest of the fatalities occurred during the evacuation preceding the storm or afterward, mostly from carbon monoxide poisoning due to misuse of gasoline-powered generators.)

Texas also has experienced three deadly epidemics, with thousands dying in outbreaks of cholera, yellow fever, and influenza during the nineteenth and early twentieth centuries.

Most nonnatural disasters in Texas have been associated with transportation. Texas has seen eleven maritime disasters (all but one of them weather-related, though ship losses are considered a separate category for this analysis), three major rail disasters, five major traffic crashes, and six aviation disasters.

Given the large role the petroleum industry has played in Texas's development, the number of oil or petrochemical disasters has been low—only four have resulted in mass casualties. Excluding wildfires, the state has had only five disastrous blazes resulting in high loss of life or widespread loss of property. Bad as Texas disasters have been, the state has never experienced a mining disaster, a killer earthquake, or a nuclear disaster.

Beyond the large number of disasters it has seen over the years, Texas holds several unfortunate distinctions:

- worst disaster in U.S. history (Galveston hurricane, 1900)
- most deadly hurricane in U.S. history (Galveston, 1900)

A stereograph image, ca. 1900, titled "Galveston Disaster.
A slightly twisted house." LIBRARY OF CONGRESS, LC-USZ62-56436

- worst railroad boiler disaster in U.S. history (San Antonio, 1912)
- worst school disaster in U.S. history (New London, 1937)
- worst industrial disaster in U.S. history (Texas City, 1947)
- worst commercial bus crash in U.S. history (McLennan County, 1952)

No matter its national ranking, disaster often becomes a catalyst for positive change. The September 8, 1900, Galveston hurricane (tropical cyclones were not named back then) killed thousands of people, but it led to the construction of a seawall that has saved hundreds if not thousands of lives since then. The storm also gave birth to a new system of municipal government, a model that spread to other cities across the nation.

The 1921 San Antonio flood resulted in the eventual transformation of the city's downtown landscape with the development of its famous river walk, now an international tourist destination.

The 1937 New London school explosion resulted in the requirement that natural gas be odorized so that leaks can be more readily detected. It also led to stricter standards for architects and engineers doing business in Texas.

The 1947 Texas City explosion brought changes in federal regulations dealing with the bagging, handling, and transport of hazardous chemicals. The harbor tragedy also heightened awareness of the need for disaster planning. Texas City and the growing tensions of the Cold War led to the establishment in 1951 of the Division of Texas Defense and Disaster Relief as a component of the Texas Department of Public Safety. (The division is now known as the Division of Emergency Management and is funded by the DPS and the governor's office.)

The 1953 Waco tornado brought about development of the nation's first storm warning system and the routine use of radar at local weather stations across the nation. The first weather-alert program began in Texas only months after the killer storm.

A quarter century later, the 1979 Wichita Falls tornado resulted in the development of storm-safe rooms in houses, another life-saving innovation.

The 1985 Delta Airlines crash led to significant improvements in wind-sheer detection at airports and more training for pilots in how to cope with these powerful downdrafts. As a result, commercial aviation is much safer.

Following Hurricane Rita, a gubernatorial task force conducted hearings to study problems associated with the chaotic mass-evacuation of Southeast Texas. A report issued in late February 2006 made numerous suggestions aimed at making a large-scale evacuation go more smoothly in future disasters.

While some measure of good came out of several of Texas's worst tragedies, other disasters caused heartbreak and havoc in the short term, only to pass into obscurity with no lingering effects on the community. Tornadoes nearly leveled Goliad and Rocksprings, for example, but today the cyclones are virtually forgotten. Transportation accidents, though they get big headlines for a time, are fairly quickly forgotten.

A devastating event may not always be remembered, but the worst usually brings out the best in Texas communities touched by disaster. As the disasters featured in this book demonstrate, every disaster has its heroes as well as its victims. In the face of adversity, Texans have tended to rise to the challenge. They help their neighbors, and they pull themselves back up as a community by their proverbial bootstraps.

With this verse from *The Sifting of Peter,* Henry Wadsworth Longfellow aptly sums up what happens to a community in the aftermath of disaster:

But noble souls, through dust and heat,
Rise from disaster and defeat
The stronger.

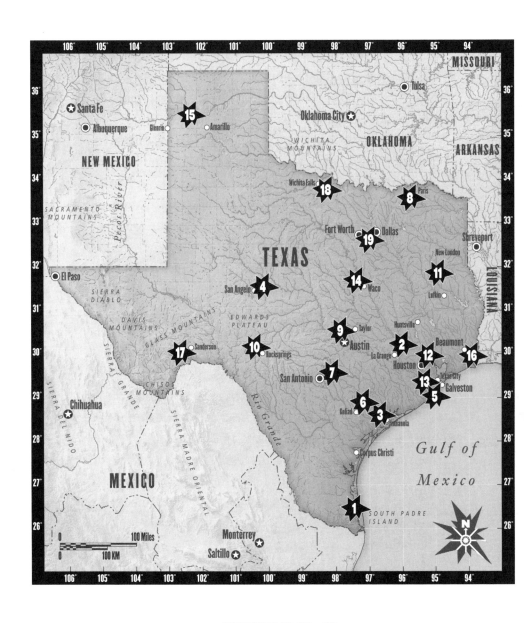

TEXAS DISASTERS

"MOST OF US WILL PERISH"

Lost Spanish Fleet

1554

On April 29, 1554, three of four gold-laden Spanish ships sailing together toward Cuba foundered and sank in a ferocious storm off the lower coast of what is now Texas. The full story of what happened on that day is unknowable, but by examining documents in Spanish archives, scholars eventually pieced together a broad outline and some reliable details. In addition, we can make some assumptions based on what happened in similar cases, in which more people survived to tell the tale. Though parts of the story below are conjecture, the event itself was real, and it stands as Texas's first major disaster.

As they secured the last of their cargo into the holds of their four-vessel *flota* for the long voyage to Spain, the sweating sailors whispered nervously. God had conferred a special power on one of five Dominicans who would be making the long voyage to Seville. According to the rumor, *Fray* Jaun Ferrer could see into the future, a gift that seemed more hellish than holy. Now, like St. Elmo's fire jumping from mast to mast on a stormy night, word spread among the seamen: Standing at the dockside, the padre had made an awful prophecy.

"Woe to those of us who are going to Spain," a Spanish chronicler some forty years later quoted the priest as saying, "because neither we nor the fleet will arrive there. Most of us will perish, and those who are left will experience great torment, though all will die in the end except a very few."

But the Crown and men of commerce with heavy investments trusted in God and the ability of their empire's seafarers to see the ships safely across the Indies from Tierra Firme—South and Central America—back to the mother country.

On April 9, 1554, with 410 men and women crowded onto four ships, the flotilla stood to sea from San Juan de Ulna, the fortified stone harborage just offshore from Veracruz. Their holds stacked to the deck above with 500-pound barrels of cochineal (the dried bodies of an insect used to produce red dye), bales of cowhides, and other items of produce from the New World, the four vessels rode low in the greenish blue water of the Gulf of Mexico. In addition to these raw materials, the ships carried more than 1.5 million pesos worth of silver and gold mined from the mountains of Mexico.

Antonio Corzo, captain-general of the small fleet, commanded from the *San Andres*. In addition to his ship, he had overall responsibility for the *Espiritu Santo,* under Damian Martin; the *San Esteban,* under Francisco del Huerto; and the *Santa Maria de Yciar,* commanded by Alonso Ojos.

Steadying himself against the rising swell as the ships cleared their dockage, Corzo ordered his helmsman to set a course to the north. Taking advantage of the current now known as the Gulf Stream, the *flota* would hug the Gulf's arching coastline to the 28th parallel (just above present-day Corpus Christi, Texas) before bearing east across the open Gulf. Off the coast of Florida, the ships would sail south for Havana, the first port of call. The typical trip to Cuba from Mexico took twenty days, but this would not be a typical voyage.

Measuring more than 70 feet from stem to stern and displacing an estimated 164 to 286 *toneladas* (Spanish ships were measured in terms of wine tons, with a *tonelada* amounting to 40 to 56 cubic feet), the armed merchant vessels under Corzo's command were the most elaborate machines of the age. Pilots standing on the ship's sterncastles used bronze astrolabes, cross-staffs, compasses, and hourglasses to determine their vessel's longitude and latitude, consulting parchment charts that showed the routes of commerce. The vessels also carried the most modern guns to protect them from French and English corsairs intent on interfering with Spanish commerce in the New World. But these sixteenth-century mariners had no instrument to help them predict the weather, as the invention of the barometer and the awareness that lower atmospheric pressure indicates an approaching storm were still nearly a century in the future.

Instead, pilots and shipmasters relied on their experience and what they learned from those who had plied the seas before them. A ring around the moon meant rain; a red sky at dawn foretold rough weather. Even the color of the ocean had meaning to men of the sea, as did the behavior of birds.

Not long after the 1554 *flota* set sail, Corzo noted the signs of an approaching storm. The seagulls, sensing the weather change, disappeared, landing to gather in white and gray flocks on the beach of the sandy island that separated what would become Texas from the Gulf. Soon the sky itself portended the coming threat, turning dark blue. The weather system came from farther out in the Gulf, a spring storm capable of churning seas of 15 feet or higher.

Anticipating a fight for survival, the captain-general probably followed the maritime custom of his age, ordering the ship's cooks to serve the best food for all aboard, regardless of class. They butchered a goat for fresh meat and bored open kegs of wine. Corzo wanted his crew fed well and fortified with strong drink, the better for what he feared lay ahead. Standing on the sterncastle, he likely addressed his subordinate officers and crew, urging their best performance for God and glory. One of the priests said Mass and took confessions. Corzo's challenge, and the measure of his art as a leader, was inspiring courage rather than fear in his men.

With God's help, Corzo knew, sailors did not stand completely defenseless in the face of a storm. When the winds rose dangerously high, he ordered his sailors to scurry topward, hauling rigging and hoisting the mainyard. If the winds continued to increase, they could take axes to the masts, chopping them down like trees and pushing them into the roiling water. Anchor chain could be dragged around the girth of the ship and made fast to hold the hulk together in battering seas. Later, when the sun came back and the sea calmed, carpenters could repair the damage and replace the mast and rigging.

But good seamanship did not always work. This spring storm, created as a late mass of cold air charged into the warm, moist air above the shallow Gulf, built huge waves. Water broke across the decks of the struggling vessels, washing some sailors to their doom.

Below deck, crew members frantically worked the bilge pumps to keep their tossing ships from taking on any more water. A chalk line on the caulked planks above them marked the point of no hope, and the water kept rising. Passengers, mostly men and women of nobility, prayed and comforted their terrified children.

The wind filling the sails of their four ships, the masters tried at first to outdistance the storm. Eventually, they simply ran out of sea room, their wallowing merchant ships heaving to in sight of the pounding surf along an alien coastline.

Maybe it was God's will, or maybe it was Corzo's skill as a master. Of the four ships, only the *San Andreas* made it through the storm to Cuba. There, the captain-general reported that the other ships of the *flota* had been wrecked "off the coast of Florida near the Rio de las Palmas at 26½ degrees." The location he described was not off modern Florida, but on the lower end of what is now known as Padre Island, a narrow, 120-mile-long barrier island stretching north from the mouth of the Rio Grande.

The equinoctial storm, a giant system generating near–hurricane-force winds, had been ferocious. It left Corzo's ship so badly damaged that the hulk had to be consigned to salvage, its cargo and treasure transferred to another vessel for the rest of the journey to Spain. As for Corzo, he later faced trial and punishment for leaving the *flota*.

Europeans had barely walked on Texas soil, but the loss of the other three Spanish ships was the state's first known disaster. Unlike most disasters, this one played out over a longer period of time. Half to two-thirds of those onboard the three ships drowned as the vessels foundered and broke up in the surf. Those who made it to the barren island's wet sand may have thanked God for their survival, but their sentiments proved premature.

His ship's masts and twisted rigging still visible above the storm-muddied water of the Gulf, the master of the *San*

Esteban and thirty of his more experienced mariners managed to salvage one of the ship's long boats. With provisions scavenged from the flotsam on the beach, Huerto and the seamen sailed south for the port of Panuco or Veracruz.

The remaining survivors, using washed-up timber and soggy sails, fashioned shelters along the beach against the burning subtropical sun. Knowing they were less than three week's sail from Veracruz, they believed they could endure the harsh environment until the joyous sight of a Spanish sail broke over the horizon.

But the survivors soon discovered that they were not alone on the coast. Behind the sand dunes and across the lagoon separating the island from the mainland, fierce bands of Indians lived. As long as the Spaniards stayed in a large group, the Indians did not attack, but they preyed on smaller parties, picking off survivors one or two at a time.

At some point the Indians managed to get between the main group of survivors and their base camp, leaving them without food or extra clothing. Whoever the survivors accepted as their leader then made a bad decision: Rather than attempt to retake their camp, they embarked to the south on foot, walking to Panuco. It became a death march.

Trailed by the Indians, the Spaniards made it to the Rio Grande. Crossing the rain-swollen stream on driftwood rafts, they swamped, losing their crossbows and the iron-tipped bolts the weapons shot. Realizing the Spaniards had lost much of their defensive edge, the Indians grew bolder, capturing some of the stragglers and stripping them of their clothes.

Seeing this, the refugees came to a bizarre conclusion: The Indians did not want to kill the Europeans because they saw them as fair-skinned aliens, perhaps demons sent by the gods. All they wanted, the Spaniards wrongly divined, was their clothing.

If an account of their journey written four decades after the fact can be believed, the Spaniards opted to take off their clothes and leave their garments as an offering to the Indians who followed them. Allowing the nude women and children to walk ahead to preserve some level of modesty, the naked Spaniards, their skin burning from solar radiation, continued south along the wild Mexican coastline.

Crazed with thirst, the women reached the next river, the Soto la Marina, ahead of the men. Lying down to drink from the river, the women may have thought their nudity exempted them from any danger from the Indians. But as they rested in the cool mud, soothing their dry throats, Indians surrounded and killed them all.

The surviving men pressed on to the next river to the south, where they soon saw Indians paddling toward them in canoes. Hoping they could hide, the Spaniards scurried into the tall grass along the bank of the stream only to be attacked by ants. Jumping into the river to get rid of the stinging insects, they found themselves at the mercy of the Indians. Only one man, *Fray* Marcos de Mena, managed to escape.

Master Huerto, meanwhile, had better luck in the long boat salvaged from the *San Esteban*. He reached Veracruz, more than 400 nautical miles from the scene of the disaster, in late May. On June 4, Viceroy Luis de Velasco approved funding for a mounted expedition to search for the wrecked ships and any survivors. The government also organized a maritime expedition. By mid-month six vessels sailed from Veracruz to salvage the wrecks.

When the commander of the rescue *entrada* made it to Panuco, he learned that the mayor of that place had already dispatched a ship to the site. When that vessel returned to port with 32,000 pesos worth of silver recovered from the *San Esteban*, the commander of the land expedition hired a ship to take him to the wreckage.

"The Lord permitted three ships to be wrecked on the 29th of [April] off the coast of Florida near the Rio de las Palmas at 26½ degrees, where more than 250 persons died and more than a million ducats were lost due to the lack of caution by pilots and sailors," a treasury official in New Spain wrote in a letter to the Crown on July 15. "Efforts are being made to recover something of what was lost."

The flotilla from Veracruz arrived on July 22. Shore parties found only unburied skeletons, but over the next two months, divers recovered roughly half of the gold and silver known to have been on the three ships.

In 1949, nearly four centuries after the disaster off Padre Island, a federally funded dredging operation began to cut through the island; the goal was to create a channel for a new seaport, a village named Port Mansfield. In the sand sucked up for this project, beachcombers began to find silver coins. Marine archaeologists later concluded that the project had destroyed the wreckage of the *Santa Maria de Yciar*.

Padre Island remained a pristine seashore, but with construction of a causeway between Port Isabel and the lower end of the island in 1954, the area began developing as a resort. As old Spanish coins continued to turn up occasionally on the shell-packed beach, word spread.

One man particularly adept at finding coins was Billy Kenon, a boat operator who lived in Port Isabel. In 1967 he teamed up with a private salvage firm from Indiana to look for the Spanish wrecks off Padre Island. Using a magnetometer, the company found a large field of scattered metal objects about a half mile out in the Gulf about 30 miles north of Port Isabel. The final resting place of the *Espiritu Santo* had been located. Kenon had developed a device that used a boat's prop wash to blow sand off the hard clay bottom of the Gulf; with this tool, divers found a treasure trove of Spanish silver and gold in addition to more prosaic but historically significant artifacts.

Texas officials soon learned what the salvagers had recovered. In December 1967 Land Commissioner Jerry Sadler asked the state attorney general's office to file suit against the Indiana company. The state contended that the artifacts were public property since the shipwreck lay in Texas waters. In state and later federal court, the legal battle lasted until 1984, when the attorney general's office and the Texas Antiquities Committee settled with the salvage firm. The Indiana company received $313,000, but Texas retained ownership of the artifacts.

Based on an extensive magnetometer survey, the Texas Antiquities Committee found the remains of the *San Esteban* in 1972. In expeditions that year and during the following summer, divers and archaeologists recovered an extensive array of artifacts—more than 12,000 kilograms of recovered items were cleaned, studied, and eventually placed in the Corpus Christi Museum. Kenon later loaned artifacts from his personal collection to Port Isabel's Treasures of the Gulf Museum.

For Texas, the value of the treasure exceeded its monetary worth. The shipwrecks were the oldest ever discovered and explored in the United States. Examination of the recovered artifacts added significant insight into the New World's maritime history. Field research coupled with archival work in Spain resulted in the publication of several books and archaeological reports.

The other lesson from the 1554 shipwrecks came not from scholarship, but from experience: Where saltwater meets the shore, the potential for disaster always exists. As *Fray* Perpetuo wrote on his way to the New World from Spain the year before the shipwrecks: "Matters of the sea are not in the hands of men."

YELLOW JACK CAME TO TEXAS

The Year of Death
1867

Governor E. M. Pease read the letter again, tears filling his eyes. His old friend in La Grange, Associate Supreme Court Justice Livingston Lindsay, had written him a two-page letter bearing hard news.

> My Dear Sir:
>
> Our mutual friend, Dr. M. Evans, and his daughter, very unexpectedly to me, and to my great surprise . . . both departed this life last night, and will be buried today. The Epidemic has not abated here, so far as there are subjects left for its actions. I have three new cases, in the last thirty-six hours, in my own family. Whether they will be fatal, I cannot judge, till further developments. . . . I don't know certainly—but it does appear to me that this favor has proved more fatal here—than it has ever been anywhere in the South, or even in the West Indies. Just to think of it—one hundred and seventy deaths, in a period of a little over four weeks, in a population, all told, of not more than 1600.

Lindsay estimated that two-thirds of the Fayette County town on the Colorado River southeast of Austin had fled to drier locations, hoping to outdistance the disease. "I am almost plain worn down," the judge concluded.

Governor Pease had the authority to call up the state militia to deal with hostile Indians or civil insurrections, but he felt powerless over the deadly epidemic then raging in his state.

From summer through the early fall of 1867, thousands of people died of yellow fever in Texas. Three thousand people fell to the disease in Galveston and Harris Counties alone. No one has ever compiled a definitive list of all those claimed by the disease during the outbreak, but both in body count and percentage of population afflicted, yellow fever exacted a staggering toll. Indeed, simply on the basis of lives lost, the epidemic stood as the state's worst disaster for nearly a third of a century.

"The year 1867 might, in Texas, be denominated the 'Year of Death,'" the Reverend Homer S. Thrall later wrote.

Yellow Jack, as some called it, had visited Texas before, but never had so many died from it. Whole families fell to the disease during the 1867 outbreak. Medical historians say that during the nineteenth century, the disease had a mortality rate of 85 percent. The 15 percent who did survive had immunity for life. But for those less fortunate, yellow fever was a cruel killer, capable of claiming even a young, healthy person within as little as three days of onset.

The first symptoms of the disease were headache, body ache, and fever. Dizziness and nausea added to the misery. Then, after about three days, many sufferers thought their prayers had been answered when they began feeling better. But the respite was like the eye of a hurricane, with the worst yet to come.

Liver damage gave victims a jaundiced appearance, hence the term "yellow" fever. The disease also attacked the kidneys and heart, causing fatty degeneration. Projectile vomiting of blood clots, a condition then called "the black vomit," added to the horror of the disease. After enduring fever-induced delirium, moribund sufferers eventually lapsed into coma. Death soon followed.

At the time, even the best medical minds thought yellow fever could be passed from human to human, that it came from "miasma," airborne particles associated with unsanitary conditions and stagnant water. Quarantines, often enforced at gunpoint, offered only false hope once the disease had surfaced in a particular community. The outbreak hit Texas's coastal cities and river towns the hardest, paying no attention to age, gender, or social status.

The 1867 epidemic is believed to have started at the busy port of Indianola, midway between Galveston and Corpus Christi. The first case occurred in Galveston, population 2,000, that June. A young man from Baltimore who had been in Indianola arrived in the Calhoun County city on June 28, started feeling badly the next day, and died on July 3. Soon the disease spread to Houston and Corpus Christi.

W. H. Maltby, editor of the *Corpus Christi Advertiser,* put out a one-page extra on August 14, 1867, listing the deaths reported as of that date. Before he started running off the edition, he set two more lines of type: "7 more deaths as we go to press, at 5 P.M." The editor wrote:

There is scarcely a house in the City that has escaped either sickness or Death. . . . Our pen is inadequate to the task of describing the distress that now prevails among us. The death of a wife and sister, the sickness of two other members of our family, and of ourself, must be the apology to our patrons for the suspension of our paper, and of this very brief notice of events that have transpired since our last issue of July 27th.

People died so frequently in Corpus Christi that, as one newspaper writer later put it, "the living could not care for the dead." Lumber delivered to build a new church instead had to be used for coffins. Families tore down fences to fashion more caskets. When wood ran out, bodies went to the grave wrapped in sheets or blankets, often three or four buried together. The same somber circumstances played out in every coastal city, from Beaumont to Brownsville.

As news of the epidemic spread, communities awaited the disease's arrival as if watching approaching storm clouds.

"To all who do not wish and do not intend to breast yellow fever," the editor of the *Brownsville Daily Ranchero* wrote, "we say get ready to leave and leave. If the port of Brazos [Santiago] shall remain open another week or two, yellow will be reported in these streets. Of this no sane man of experience can entertain a doubt."

The disease also spread upriver into the interior of the state, particularly along the more populated Trinity, Brazos, and Colorado watersheds. "At every little town within fifty or one hundred miles of the coast the disease has found its way," the Brownsville newspaper reported.

Washington County, on the east side of the Brazos, suffered enormously during the epidemic. The terror the disease generated is typified in the story of Benjamin R. Thomas, who came to Texas from North Carolina in 1836. After the Texas

Revolution, he settled in Washington County, married, and took up farming.

As a Texas Ranger, Thomas had protected Texans from hostile Comanches, but he could not save his family from yellow fever. His fifty-seven-year-old wife, Mary, died on September 15, soon followed by his son.

Thomas's step-son, Robert Elgin, had joined the Confederate Army at nineteen, serving through the Civil War in the Eighth Texas Cavalry, better known as Terry's Texas Rangers. Surviving some of the war's toughest fighting, he came back to Washington County at war's end. By December 1866 he had courted and won the hand of seventeen-year-old Mary Virginia Stanchfield, the daughter of a wealthy Chappell Hill planter.

On August 26, 1867, Mary gave birth to their first child, a boy they named after his father. Then Yellow Jack came to town. Only twenty-five, Robert Elgin died on October 1. Eighteen-year-old Mary joined him in death the following day. Little Robert Elgin Jr. lasted only five more days.

Another Washington County resident was the widow of Sam Houston, former state governor and president of the Republic of Texas. Margaret Lea had moved to Independence from Huntsville after her husband's death in July 1863. Life had been hard on the forty-eight-year-old woman since she lost her famous husband, but her religious convictions and her children sustained her.

By October, Independence had withered to a virtual ghost town. Baylor College had been shut down. As a warning to the healthy, white sheets hung from the houses of those who had come down with the disease.

Hoping to avoid the harmful vapors believed to cause the fever, Margaret stayed inside with her children as much as she could. After receiving word that her older daughter Maggie was coming to visit, Margaret opted to travel to her daughter's residence at Labadie Prairie so that Maggie would not be exposed to the disease then ravaging Independence. Even after she heard that the disease seemed to have run its course in Washington County, Margaret decided to go stay with another daughter at Georgetown, in Central Texas.

Stopping by Independence only long enough to pick up some things prior to the westward journey, Margaret felt the slight sting of a mosquito bite. She thought nothing of it, but soon she became sick. A second wave of the epidemic had begun. Realization of that caused justifiable panic. Riders galloped out of town, followed by buggies and wagons as people cried out, "Yellow Fever! Yellow Fever!"

But the warning had come too late for Margaret. She died on December 3, 1867, after two days of delirium. Wary of getting sick themselves, no one was willing to take the body of Houston's widow to Huntsville for burial at her husband's side. Instead, she went into a deeper-than-normal grave outside Independence. Margaret had been a very religious woman, but the local Baptist preacher would not even preside at her brief funeral for fear of infection.

Conditions in Huntsville stood just as grim, the disease claiming one out of ten residents. On October 2, a young married woman named M. Thornton, still recovering from an attack of the fever, wrote her cousins to describe conditions in Huntsville. "In some families, six out of seven have been taken," she wrote, "and half of the time there is no one to lay them out or to go to see them buried."

Her husband and children had survived their bout with the disease, she continued, but "all my best friends are gone. . . .

There is no business going on of any kind but Coffin making and grave digging."

Few Texans of the time would not have known at least someone who died. In a 1903 article, the *Austin Statesman* reported:

> For months a great pall of gloom hung over the entire state. Thousands of homes were in mourning. Not a day passed but what deaths were announced by the score, and sometimes by the hundred. Business was almost entirely suspended. Merchants left their stores to return and find the stock of provisions consumed, by whom they have never known.
>
> They were uncomplaining, however, because they felt they had been used to mitigate suffering in the supremest exigency Texas ever knew.

Corpus Christi had 300 deaths, almost a third of its population. Indianola reported at least seventy-five deaths. Inland, La Grange had 204 deaths, nearly a fifth of its population. In Brenham, the seat of Washington County, yellow fever afflicted 40 percent of the population, killing 500 residents. By September 17, the *Houston Telegraph and Texas Register* reported thirty-seven deaths out of seventy cases reported in Hempstead.

The epidemic may be one of the reasons that the state population increase from 1860 to 1870 (604,215 residents to 818,579) was the smallest recorded since the U.S. Census Bureau began its count in Texas.

The epidemic killed towns as well as people. Places like Millican in Brazos County and Chappell Hill in nearby Washington County never really recovered from the epidemic. Until shortly before the outbreak, Millican had been the largest town in Texas north of Houston, but a combination of the end of its status as a railhead and the epidemic relegated it to virtual ghost-town status in only a few years.

"Yellow fever is in our midst," Millican's postmaster wrote to the *Houston Daily Telegram* on September 14, "four deaths have already occurred and several more cases exist. The citizens are badly frightened, all who can, have left; twill be useless to send mail matter to this place . . . as no one will be here to receive it. I have my goods back & am ready to leave, will send you notice upon my return. . . . Please inform citizens."

A few days later the *Galveston Daily News* reported that the Millican postmaster had "fled to the woods & the telegraph operator is dead."

Not everyone tried to outrun the disease. Doctors heroically ministered to the sufferers. Unable to cure the afflicted, they did what they could to make their patients comfortable. By staying in an area experiencing an outbreak, many doctors contracted the disease themselves and died. The disease claimed Corpus Christi's only two physicians.

The other heroes of the 1867 epidemic were the members of Howard associations, composed mainly of men and women who had survived the disease and become immune. Named for British philanthropist John Howard (1726–1790), the first such organization began in Boston in 1812. These autonomous citizen associations spread across the nation and into Texas, where the first group organized in Galveston in 1844 to deal with a yellow fever outbreak. Howard associations in Galveston and Corpus Christi raised money to help the families of the afflicted, provided nursing care and moral support, and coordinated burials.

*Reproduction of a painting by Dean Cornwell showing yellow fever experiments
in which Dr. Jesse W. Lazear inoculated Dr. James Carroll with an infected
mosquito at a U.S. Army hospital in Havana, Cuba, in 1900.*
LIBRARY OF CONGRESS, PRINTS & PHOTOGRAPHS DIVISION, LC-USZ62-119807

When the air freshened and cooled that fall, Texans knew
that the scourge would be ending soon. Yellow fever hit Texas
again in 1873 and 1878, though neither of these outbreaks
equaled the 1867 epidemic. It was another four decades before
doctors understood that it was not "miasma" that transmitted
the disease but a creature long considered annoying but certainly not deadly: the mosquito.

In 1881 a Cuban doctor, Carlos Juan Finlay, presented a paper to the Royal Academy in Havana suggesting that mosquitoes, not humans, could be the carrier of the disease. But final proof did not come until August 31, 1900, when Dr. James Carroll, a member of Dr. Walter Reed's Yellow Fever Commission, came down with the disease after having been bitten by a mosquito four days earlier.

With the realization that mosquitoes transmitted the virus responsible for the disease, health officials attacked the problem by eliminating mosquito habitats and urging people to wear protective clothing and use netting to avoid being bitten. The medical community still had no pharmacological way to prevent the disease, but with improved sanitation, no epidemics occurred in Texas after 1907. Nearly another forty years went by before medical science developed a vaccine to prevent the disease, though there still is no curative treatment for those who contract the virus.

Outside of genealogists and historians, few twenty-first-century Texans are aware of the deadly disaster that swept their state during Reconstruction. But many a weathered tombstone in Texas shows that the grave's occupant died in 1867, the state's "Year of Death."

"THE TOWN IS GONE"

Indianola Hurricanes
1875 and 1886

Sitting at their rolltop desks penning articles for the next edition, the staff of the *Galveston Daily News* had no shortage of
local news on September 21, 1875. Less than a week before,
their city had taken a glancing blow from a powerful hurricane.
Caught in the storm, the steamship *City of Waco* had gone
down in the bay with the loss of fifty-five souls. But Galveston
had been on the fringe of the storm, which the U.S. Army Signal Service now believed had done its worst damage farther
down the coast from the prosperous island port.

Suddenly, the tempo of city sounds coming through the
Daily News building's open window changed. Looking outside
the window to see what all the commotion was about, Editor-
in-Chief D. C. Jenkins saw people hurrying toward the docks.
He and others in the building quickly joined the crowd and
soon heard the news: A ship flying her flag at half-staff had
cleared the sandbar at the entrance to the bay.

Onlookers ranging from bankers to dray drivers stood anx-
iously on the pier as crew members of the *Harlan,* one of the
Morgan Line's steamships, tossed their lines. They knew

something tragic had happened. Then someone shouted stunning news. Indianola, 150 miles down coast from Galveston, had been devastated by the hurricane. Scores had been killed, and many others were reported missing.

The *Harlan*'s master hurried ashore and personally delivered a letter to the newspaper from W. H. (Jim) Crain, the district attorney in Indianola.

"We are destitute," the hastily written message began. "The town is gone. One-tenth of the population . . . gone. Dead bodies are strewn for twenty miles along the bay. Nine-tenths of the houses are destroyed. Send us help, for God's sake."

The *Harlan*'s arrival confirmed what had been a growing concern. With the telegraph connection to Indianola dead, Galvestonians had assumed that the worst of the storm must have been toward the middle of the coast. Nothing had been heard from Indianola since September 15, the day the storm had battered Galveston with gale-force winds, heavy rain, and high water.

Soon more grim news made its way to Galveston. "Many of our acquaintances and friends are drowned," Indianola businessman Henry Seeligson wrote. "The writer is thoroughly exhausted, having been out with a burying party all last night, but will have to go down the bay this evening again to bury others."

In 1875 an estimated 5,000 people lived in Indianola, a city on Matagorda Bay. As the state's second-busiest port, Indianola enjoyed a flourishing commerce. But proximity to the sea comes with a high price.

On Wednesday, September 15, Indianola had bustled with more than the normal level of activity. A spectacular murder trial was under way at the Calhoun County courthouse, with

Bill Taylor facing a possible death sentence for the March 11, 1874, shooting in Indianola of William Sutton and his friend Gabriel Slaughter. The killing had been the most recent outbreak of violence in an ongoing grudgefest that came to be known as the Sutton-Taylor feud. With partisans of both factions in town for the trial, tension ran high.

But as lawyers prepared their opening arguments, trouble of another sort bore down on Indianola. Through telegraphic reports, the U.S. Army's Signal Service headquarters in Washington had been following the progress of a tropical cyclone that had blown past Haiti and Cuba and now churned somewhere in the Gulf of Mexico.

As testimony continued in the Taylor trial, a strong wind blew from the east. Atmospheric moisture created a halo around the sun before it disappeared. Under a gray sky, the barometric pressure began dropping. Clearly the coast was in for a blow, but no one in Indianola seemed particularly concerned.

That changed on Thursday morning, when heavy waves broke on a normally placid bay shore. The wind began to howl, and by noon water surged across Main Street "like a mill race." Using rowboats, people began relocating to the northern side of town as businessmen removed cash and assorted valuables from their safes. The barometer continued to fall.

Planks from what had been Indianola's wharves now battered against the sides of buildings in the ever-rising storm surge. Soon the buildings along Water Street began collapsing.

People needed to get to higher ground. But the storm surge had already cut off the roads. At the railroad station a passenger train sat on the tracks, unable to get out of town; its steam boiler had been drained and could not be refilled because salt water had washed into the depot's cistern.

Even with water covering the floor of the jail, Sheriff F. L. Busch refused to move the prisoners, including Taylor. District Attorney Crain, thinking Taylor more properly deserved hanging than drowning, took the keys from the sheriff's office and let Taylor and two other prisoners out on their promise that they would not try to escape.

A short time later, with deputies preoccupied by the worsening storm, Taylor broke his promise, fleeing town on stolen horses. After reaching higher ground, the accused murderer thoughtfully left the horse behind and proceeded on foot.

Though Taylor had only his own safety in mind, others did all they could to save their fellow townspeople. Jim Crain had fought Yankees during the Civil War as a soldier in Terry's Texas Rangers. Astride a big, black horse, he carried as many people as he could to higher ground. Struggling to hold onto his strong horse, people clutched Crain's saddle and stirrups. Some clung to the horse's tail as the veteran cavalryman half-swam his mount to safety.

Seeligson also rode his horse through the wind-blown rain, his face stinging like he had been slapped. Finally making it to his house, he jumped from the exhausted animal and put his family in a wagon, still hoping to make it to higher ground. After only a few blocks, he realized he could go no farther.

"The waters were . . . full six feet deep and running at a fearful rate," he later recalled. Somehow, he and his family made it to the courthouse, where they rode out the storm.

Elsewhere in town, many people were not as fortunate. From the sturdy, stone courthouse, Seeligson and others watched as the storm swept a building with more than thirty people inside out into the wild waters of Powderhorn Bayou. Two-thirds of them drowned.

View of Indianola from the bay on the Royal Yard onboard the barque Texana, *September 1860 (drawn from nature by Helmuth Holtz). Before the hurricane, Indianola was a thriving port city. After the hurricane, only eight buildings remained.* LIBRARY OF CONGRESS, PRINTS & PHOTOGRAPHS DIVISION, LC-USZC4-2778

Suddenly the water broke through the door of the courthouse, forcing the Seeligsons and everyone else inside to scurry upstairs to the second floor.

"The building, although constructed . . . of the stoutest masonry, with foundation six feet deep and five in diameter, rocked as though an earthquake was in progress," Seeligson remembered. "The rushing of the waters through the lower doors and windows and the [wind] was so deafening that one could scarcely hear his own voice."

The most tragic news story of his career swirling around him, *Indianola Bulletin* editor C. A. Ogsbury had to think of his family first. With his wife and two children and his mother-in-law, he watched the devastation from the second-floor window of neighbor R. D. Martin's residence. "The situation was awful,"

Ogsbury later wrote. "Screams from women and children could be heard in every direction."

At 5 P.M. that day, Sergeant C. A. Smith recorded a barometric reading of 28.90 and a wind speed of 82 mph. Fifteen minutes later the cups of the anemometer blew away, the last reading showing 86 mph.

Early Friday morning the winds finally died down as the hurricane moved farther inland. When the storm surge receded, Indianola lay in ruins. Only eight buildings, one of them being the courthouse, had survived the wind and water. Bodies lay scattered as far as 20 miles from town, along with dead livestock and pets.

An estimated 270 persons died in the storm, but with Indianola cut off from the rest of the state, it took a while for news of the tragedy to spread. The first ship to reach the wrecked city, the *Harlan,* immediately made for Galveston with the district attorney's urgent plea for help.

After a twelve-hour ride, a reporter for the Victoria newspaper finally reached Indianola at 9 A.M. on Sunday, September 19. Based on the journalist's dispatches, the *Advocate* hit the streets with this stacked headline:

> Indianola!
> Thursday's Storm!
> A Day of Danger
> And Night of Horror!

"It is difficult even to identify where many of the buildings [had] stood," the article reported.

Indianola rebuilt, but it never fully recovered from the 1875 storm. And eleven years later another hurricane devastated the port city.

On August 18, 1886, Signal Service observer Isaac Reed received a wire from Washington: A hurricane had entered the Gulf of Mexico and likely would bring gale force winds to the eastern Gulf coast. Indianola being on the western side of the Gulf, the government did not order Reed to raise his station's storm flag.

That instruction did come the following day, but by then, it made no real difference. Although a minimal hurricane, the storm caused maximum damage to Indianola. "Buildings which stoutly withstood the great cyclone of 1875, went down as if made of pasteboard," the *Victoria Advocate* reported eight days later.

As had been the case eleven years before, Indianola had no shortage of heroes.

Captain Reed stayed in the Signal Service station all night, recording the rising wind and falling barometric pressure and telegraphing the numbers to Washington.

John S. Munn, an attorney from Victoria, had been in town that Thursday for a court case. The howling of a cat awakened him shortly after 1 A.M. on Friday. "A seething, foaming torrent passed through the streets," he recalled, "buildings tottered for a moment, trembled, groaned, and in a twinkling disappeared in the spray and darkness." Leaving his hotel, Munn made his way across town. "The spray cut the flesh like shot," he said.

"Boys, come up and help me close the back door," he heard Captain Reed shout from the building that housed his office. Inside, Munn found Reed still taking observations by the light of a lamp as telegraph operator L. H. Woodworth tapped out the numbers. Also riding out the storm in the frame government building were Dr. H. Rosencranz, T. D. Woodward of the U.S. Customs Service, and W. J. Morrison.

Indianola after the 1886 hurricane.
COURTESY OF THE CALHOUN COUNTY MUSEUM AND THE ROSEATE SPOONBILL GALLERY, PORT LAVACA

"Great goodness," Munn heard Caption Reed shout over the wind. "The barometer is still falling." The captain said he would screw down the anemograph, "so that if the office goes and I am lost it may be found and read."

When the building began to move, Munn and the others decided they needed to get out. Tony Lagus's nearby grocery seemed like a safer structure.

"The water is up to my waist at my house," Reed said. "My family may be lost but my post of duty is here." As Munn left, he and the others argued that Reed had better get out. The building continued to shake. The captain finally relented to their arguments and said he would be along shortly; the doctor decided to wait with him.

Just as the two men finally walked out of the building, it fell down, pinning them under heavy lumber.

Reed had been correct in that his house was full of salt water—7 feet deep, to be exact—but his wife and family survived. The captain did not.

"Your dear papa was drowned in a terrible cyclone at 6 o'clock on the morning of the 19th," Alice Reed wrote a son who had been away at the time. "The building falling forward, he was caught under it. When they came down out of the office they left a lamp burning; it upset, [and] caught fire."

Whipped by the fierce winds, the fire rapidly intensified.

"We stopped for a while," Munn recalled, "and gazed with horror on this unexpected danger. It was then that the ladies shed tears, every lip faltered, every cheek blanched, how were it then possible to escape death[?]"

At that point, Munn continued, one woman said, "Well, I guess we have our choice, to be drowned or roasted."

Quickly spreading from the Signal Service office, the fire raced through every building on its side of the street, including August Frank's warehouse, the Lagus grocery store, Steinbach's market, and a liquor store. Jumping across the street, the flames consumed a hotel, a bakery, a dry-goods store, a drug store, a private residence, and other buildings.

"The howling blast, the roaring sea, the crash of falling timbers, the explosion of [gun] powder in stores, the crackling of flames as they shot up from, and lapped over the doomed buildings which rapidly yielded to wind, wave and fire, tottered, quivered and shrieking, fell into ruins and disappeared," Munn wrote breathlessly.

This time no one wanted to rebuild in Indianola.

County residents voted 188 to 7 on November 2, 1886, to move the Calhoun County seat to Port Lavaca, located on a high bluff. The following April a fire destroyed the few buildings the hurricane had left standing. On May 7, 1887, the federal government announced that it intended to close Indianola's post office.

In the early 1900s it was a common day trip to go down to the ruins and picnic in the old city.   COURTESY OF THE CALHOUN COUNTY MUSEUM AND THE ROSEATE SPOONBILL GALLERY, PORT LAVACA

Galveston had been the first city to organize a relief party for Indianola after the 1875 storm, and its citizens contributed money again after the 1886 hurricane. No one in Galveston or anywhere else wished Indianola ill, but the island city certainly profited from its rival's demise.

Galveston could have profited in another, much more important way, had it chosen to. The tragedy at Indianola, the *Galveston Daily News* observed, "teaches us the importance of fortifying the beach against the assaults of the terrible Gulf breakers, which are dangerous at 35 miles per hour." The newspaper article went on to envision a system of 5-foot brick walls, high enough above sea level to keep a tidal surge from sweeping the city's streets as had twice been the case in Indianola. "As the city's [Galveston] permanent prosperity has been doubly assured by the late storm," the newspaper continued, "let the work be—first, durable, and next, speedy."

Such a project would cost Galveston $180,000 "for the most needy part of the city," the newspaper estimated. Unfortunately, nothing came of the proposal.

Fourteen years later a storm destroyed much of the town, forcing Galveston to adopt even more drastic measures of protecting itself from Indianola's fate.

"ALL WASHED AWAY"

Ben Ficklin Flood
1882

Bigger than some states, Tom Green County stretched across West Texas all the way to New Mexico. It had a lot of land but not very many residents. When federal census enumerators moved through the county in 1880, they counted only 3,609 people.

But anyone who gave it much thought knew that the area had a promising future. The army and the Texas Rangers had just about eliminated the threat of hostile Indians, and it would not be long before the railroad came. In only a few years, the more visionary believed, West Texas would be covered with prosperous ranches and thriving cities. One of those cities would be Ben Ficklin.

The town was named for Benjamin Franklin Ficklin, a Confederate veteran from Virginia who won a contract to carry mail from Fort Smith, Arkansas, to San Antonio, with a branch line to El Paso. In 1869, setting up stopping places for his stagecoaches, Ficklin bought a square mile of land on the east side of the South Concho River, 3.5 miles downstream from Fort Concho, a cavalry post established two years before. Ficklin sent his good friend and business associate Francis C. Taylor to operate what became known as the Concho Mail Station. Taylor's brother Blake and his sister, Mrs. M. J. Metcalfe, moved there, too. Mrs. Metcalfe had a son, Charles, and daughters Fannie, Zemula, and Amelia.

When Ficklin died accidentally in 1871, Taylor and two partners took over the stage line. A couple of years later, they had a town site surveyed about a mile downstream from the stagecoach station. Taylor named the new community Ben Ficklin in honor of his late friend. The legislature created Tom Green County in March 1874, and Ben Ficklin became county seat in 1875.

Ben Ficklin's principal commercial rival was San Angela, a somewhat smaller town just across the river from Fort Concho. Soldiers, buffalo hunters, and cowboys afforded the proprietors of the town's saloons, gaming establishments, and bawdy houses a brisk business. San Angela was not exactly Sodom and Gomorrah, but the people who lived in Ben Ficklin grew a bit high-minded about their community.

Some in San Angela, meanwhile, aspired to better things. If San Angela could get a post office or become the county seat, it would do a lot better in the long run. Someone carped that Ben Ficklin should never have been built, adding to the slander with the observation that the town "was needed on the Concho [about] as badly as [stage operator Taylor's] Concord coach needed a fifth wheel."

No matter the sentiments of its jealous neighbors, Ben Ficklin rolled along just fine with nearly 800 residents supporting numerous businesses. In 1881 voters approved construction of an $18,000, two-story stone courthouse to replace the much less impressive structure that housed the county's offices. Knowing that taxpayers would not want to see public money wasted by moving the county seat to San Angela, the movers and shakers of Ben Ficklin figured they had assured their town's continuing prosperity. But the people of Ben Ficklin would soon learn that a community's long-term health depended on more than demographics, reputation, or political acumen.

The spring and summer of 1882 had been unusually wet for West Texas. Even in the dog days of August, cool, clear water ran through draws into the three forks of the Concho. The grass had stayed green and cattle were fat. Late in the afternoon of August 23, a towering thunderstorm swept from the northwest toward Ben Ficklin. The rain started around 9 P.M. and "came in torrents for more than an hour," as the *Tom Green County Times* later reported. That storm passed, but an hour later another giant thunderhead loomed over Ben Ficklin. Again, rain came down hard. "The thunder which pealed across the skies made sleep impossible," the newspaper continued. As the water beat down on their roofs, some residents began to get uneasy about "to-morrow and what to-morrow would reveal," as the *Times* put it. "All night it continued its impetuous fall."

Overnight nearly 7 inches of rain fell over the Concho River's watershed. By early morning the middle and south forks flowed 200 to 300 hundred feet wide and the water continued to rise. It also kept raining. "The rain poured," the *Times* reported. "It seemed to have come for all time." When the rain finally let up at 11 A.M., the normally shallow South Concho ran 40 feet deep, washing Ben Ficklin away.

A big man with mild blue eyes, F. A. Karger had been in Ben Ficklin since 1875. He worked as a farrier at the Concho

Mail Station but quit when he realized that the coming of the Texas & Pacific Railroad would mean the end of the stagecoach business. Karger liked living on the Concho and had opened his own blacksmith shop there.

Things went well for him until that summer of 1882 when the storm came.

As the water began to rise, Karger managed to get to higher ground. Out of danger, he watched as everything he owned disappeared down the river in the swirling red water. "Chairs, goods, trunks, boxes and furniture of all kinds," the newspaper later reported, rushed from the town and from ranch houses upstream from Ben Ficklin. The sound of gunfire from the courthouse diverted Karger's attention from his loss. Karger could not imagine why someone would be shooting.

Later he learned that H. B. Tarver, the county surveyor, had been trapped on the viewing area outside the building's narrow dome, the highest spot in town. The surveyor had watched in amazement as the water steadily climbed the sides of the building. Then his fascination shifted to fervent prayer that the building's walls would withstand the force of the raging floodwaters. Convinced that that whole building soon would be underwater, he discharged his six-shooter in the air, hoping someone would rescue him. But no one could get to the building through the fast-moving water.

Earlier, with floodwaters battering the door of the county jail, a young cowboy named Clint Johnson and a few helpers liberated thirteen prisoners from the lockup. Most of those behind bars had been incarcerated for public intoxication, but one accused murderer got a chance to cheat the hangman's noose if he survived the flood. After freeing the prisoners, Johnson had to climb a tree to keep from being washed away.

Also thinking of others, C. D. Foote raced in his buggy to the stage station to urge the people there to get to higher ground. The land agent loaded eight people in his wagon, but Foote could not convince Mrs. Metcalfe—Taylor's sister—to leave. She had seen the river get up before, and she believed that it had risen about as high as it would. Her daughter Zemula said she would stay with her mother. Also remaining were Mrs. Metcalfe's brother, Blake Taylor, along with S. C. Robertson, George Robinson, and a couple of hired hands.

When the water continued to rise, Mrs. Metcalfe finally comprehended the extent of the danger. Everyone tried to leave in Robertson's hack, but his team, frightened by the water, refused to budge. Now their only choice was climbing onto the roof of the station until the water went down.

On the basis of Foote's report that Mrs. Metcalfe and her daughter had stayed at the stage station, two men in a rowboat set out from Ben Ficklin, hoping to rescue the group. When Terrell Harris and Kerby Smith reached the station, however, their boat swamped. The two men swam to a grove of pecan trees and climbed up the tallest one. From their perch they saw the fast-moving water cut the roof of the stage stop in half, each portion swirling down the river with its human occupants desperately trying to cling to the lumber. As the two would-be rescuers watched, everyone but Robertson, who had managed to make it to one of the pecan trees, disappeared under the raging water.

Seeing another woman clinging to a tree surrounded by water, Clifton Gill and Ben Mayes took off their clothes and swam to her aid. When the woman saw that the young men were naked, she refused to get out of the tree until they got dressed. Gill obligingly swam back to the riverbank, donned his clothes, and swam back out. This time the woman allowed herself to be rescued.

Before long Gill needed rescuing himself. He and three others had taken refuge on a rooftop, but a floating tree smashed the roof, sending everyone into the water. The next day two cowboys found Gill in the top of a pecan tree still surrounded by flood waters.

The August 26 issue of the *Tom Green County Times* ran with black borders between the four columns of type on page one. "Terrific Flood!" the five-deck headline began, followed by "Great Destruction of Life. Thousands of Dollars Lost in the Seething Waters. Ben Ficklin Almost Wholly Ruined, And San Angela Partially Inundated. Some Particulars of the Disaster." Making no pretense of journalistic objectivity, the editor concluded, "Our report closes as we go to press. Such sickening details and horrid suspicions of death we do not often meet in life. . . . As it is we feel relief in closing the initial chapter of so terrible a calamity."

Three days after the flood, rancher David Williams sat down to write his sister. "I sent you a letter only a few days ago," he began, "but I write you again so soon, thinking perhaps you may see accounts in the papers of the terrible calamity which has befallen this part of the country, and may feel some anxiety concerning our safety."

Ben Ficklin, he said, "is swept away, many lives have been lost, and a large amount of property destroyed.

"It was a forty foot rise," he continued, "and came up at the rate of an inch per minute. Ben Ficklin was built mostly on a flat at an elevation of twenty-five feet above the river. . . . Only the two courthouses (old and new), and the county jail now remain. These are rock buildings, and very substantially built.

Other rock buildings were swept entirely away. The water was fifteen feet in the courthouse and all through the town, except a few dwellings up on the hill, which were spared."

The flood made national news. "Ben Ficklin is all washed away except eight houses," the *New York Times* reported. "The country presents a spectacle which beggars description. Houses, horses, cattle, and clothing are piled up in heaps at every step."

When the magnitude of the tragedy sank in, the people of San Angela did all they could for their formal rivals. "Parties from all sections of the county came forward and offered every assistance," the *Times* reported. "Messrs. Foote, Lackey, and W.H. Lessing opened their [business] houses and said, 'take what we have.'" At a public meeting on August 28, San Angelans passed their cowboy hats and collected $4,000 for their neighbors. The military garrison at Fort Concho also did its part, with the Sixteenth Infantry's band performing a benefit concert.

Sixty-five bodies eventually were found, but likely more people died in the flood. As Williams wrote his sister, "Probably many never will be found, as there are such enormous piles of drift, in which bodies are hidden. I guess from all I can learn, a majority of those lost were Mexicans. The loss of life in Tom Green Co. is somewhere from eighty to one hundred persons. I doubt if we ever find out just how many."

Ben Ficklin had a small cemetery, but it and most of its occupants washed away in the flood. Charles B. Metcalfe, one of Taylor's nephews, picked a new location for the graveyard—this time on higher ground. He saw to the reburial of those whose remains had been exposed by the flood, including his uncle. The new cemetery also served as the burial place for most of the victims of the flood, including Metcalfe's mother, sister, and uncle Blake.

Beyond the human toll, property loss in Ben Ficklin was estimated at more than $115,000. Losses reported elsewhere in the county came to an additional $70,000. Hundreds of sheep, cattle, and horses also drowned in the torrent, their bloated bodies marring the landscape for miles downstream.

What Williams saw and heard impacted him greatly. "I heard a sermon preached today, for the first time in four years and seven months," the cowboy confided to his sister.

Though the survivors prayed for those who had been lost and gave thanks that they had been spared, the flood killed the spirit of the town. A few people hung on, but most of the survivors moved to nearby San Angela, which had fared much better in the deluge. Backwater pushed up the North Concho by the flow from the South Concho flooded some low-lying areas, but nothing on the scale of what had happened in Ben Ficklin.

The September 2 issue of the *Tom Green County Times* carried several advertisements like these:

W.H. Brown: Late of Ben Ficklin would respectfully inform his friends, also the public in general, that he has moved to San Angela and can be found at the Blue Ribbon Saloon, where he will supply the best of Wines, Liquors, and Cigars to his patrons.

And, John Engel, "late of Ben Ficklin . . . respectfully informs his friends and the public that he has removed from the washout, and may now be found at Keyer's old store on Oakes Street."

Land agent C. D. Foote also correctly assumed business would no longer be brisk in Ben Ficklin. He notified the public that due to "an unprecedented calamity [having] overwhelmed the village of Ben Ficklin . . . as soon as my office can be fitted up, I will resume business in the town of San Angela, where my clients will please address me."

Indeed, as Williams wrote on September 10 in another letter to his sister, "Ben Ficklin will never be rebuilt. The families have all moved to San Angela, and Ft. Concho, and the county seat will be at Concho too as soon as we can have an election, and make the change."

In its September 16 edition, the county newspaper reported: "Our streets have been lined with freight wagons, and vehicles of every description bringing people into San Angela to make their purchases. Lumber has commenced to arrive and many buildings are being erected." Jonathan Miles had a new addition platted on the north end of town and offered a free lot to anyone who had survived the flood.

Less than a year later, Tom Green County voters overwhelmingly approved the removal of the county seat to San Angela, where the newly designated post office was renamed San Angelo by some Washington bureaucrat. By 1884 San Angelo had a new stone courthouse and what little remained of Ben Ficklin had become a ghost town.

A CITY IN RUINS

Galveston Hurricane
1900

Eight-year-old Sarah Helen Littlejohn busily played dolls with her friend and neighbor, Minnie Lee Borden, in a second-floor bedroom. The children probably would have been outside that Saturday morning, September 8, 1900, if not for the rain that had started the previous evening.

Sarah's oldest sister came upstairs with news: "Papa's home." Elbridge Gerry Littlejohn, a teacher and the principal of the Broadway school in Galveston, had been downtown visiting and tending to business. Saturday marked the end of a full six-day workweek. Men took time for drinking coffee and talking commerce.

With a population of 38,000 in 1900, Galveston was one of the busiest ports and richest cities in the United States. The city could—and did—boast of its modern amenities: the state's first telephone and first building with electric lighting, prize-winning architecture, the Grand Opera House, and high society. Galveston also had the *Daily News,* the state's oldest continuing newspaper and one of the best journals in any city of its size, anywhere.

The weather was another matter. Galveston Island had been troubled by damaging tropical storms throughout its history, and another now bore down on the city. While most islanders retreated from the rainstorm, angry waves lashing the beach attracted sightseers from the mainland who came by rail or boat to see it for themselves. Some foolhardy men even attempted to ride the waves.

Alarmed by a report from local climatologist Isaac Cline, Littlejohn went home around noon. All over Galveston men began leaving their shops and offices to go home and check on the safety of their families. Littlejohn told his wife, Helen, and the children that the pagoda had washed away. The Beach Hotel's pagoda, a popular landmark that extended over the water and was shaped like an Oriental temple, was a bathhouse for swimmers. Wind and waves had shattered the buildings and piers.

The rain, driven by a strong wind, quickly submerged lower parts of Galveston Island. Streetcar tracks washed out. Telephone wires snapped in the wind. Here and there dray horses lost their footing and panicked. Fighting against their entangling harnesses and trace chains, they tried to swim the powerful current.

Already the rising water lapped only a block from the Littlejohns' west-side home on Avenue O.

By noon the winds began to swing around from the east. The tide crept onto the sand past the low-lying areas and into homes nearest the Gulf. The storm that was about to come ashore on Galveston Island had already slammed into the Florida coast. But because the storm left Florida without telegraphic service, the U.S. Weather Bureau station in Galveston had received no warning of the approaching tropical cyclone.

On his own initiative, Cline hoisted the hurricane-warning flags. By midafternoon the weather office's rain gauge blew away, followed shortly by the anemometer, which had recorded gusts of 100 mph.

Convinced that he could do nothing more, Cline went home to be with his family. His wife, Cora Mae, was in her fourth pregnancy and not doing well.

Joseph Cline, Isaac's brother and also a climatologist, attempted but failed to telegraph a report to Washington. Instead Joseph used the island's long-distance operator to telephone the Western Union office in Houston and instruct them to telegraph the government weather bureau in Washington.

Then Joseph went to his brother's house.

That evening outside their living room window, the Littlejohn family spotted an old man half-swimming, half-wading through high water. They brought him inside and soon discovered that he was German and spoke little English. Sarah later remembered: "It seemed to me that he could not understand us, for it took mamma a very long time to make him come in. . . . It surely did sound funny to hear him talk. He said he did not mind the water, but it was the wind he did not like. He was an old fisherman."

All over the island, people shared whatever shelter they could find.

Some fifty of Isaac Cline's neighbors sought out the second floor of his house, certain it would be safe. Joseph argued that the center of town would be safer, but Isaac stood firm. Soon Isaac, his pregnant wife, his three daughters, Joseph, and their neighbors crowded together and listened to the terrifying sounds of a city being torn apart.

Some people rode out the storm alone.

Thomas McGown had taken shelter in his third-floor office. The city no longer had electricity, but most islanders kept lamps and candles on hand for emergencies. In a letter addressed to his brother George McGown of Fort Worth, Thomas wrote:

> I can't go to sleep while it is blowing like it is. There is right now (9 o'clock P.M.) about four feet of water all over the island, and it is still coming up. I am up in my office and when I tell you that the water is over my head down on the sidewalks (not in the street) I am not exaggerating one bit, for I just went down the steps until I was up to my neck in water and did not get to the sidewalk. . . . To try to tell you anything of the storm, or scene this afternoon is just impossible.

Saturday night the storm surge flooded the low-lying island. Unable to escape, many frightened families climbed to the second or third floor of their houses or buildings. Others clung to the rooftops of houses already blown from their foundations.

As the Cline house collapsed, Joseph gripped the hands of two of his nieces and jumped to safety. His brother, sister-in-law, and friends who had taken shelter from the storm were swept away. Isaac clutched his youngest daughter and survived in the black, surging, debris-filled flood. The brothers found one another and clung to a raft of floating wreckage. But neither Isaac nor Joseph could find Cora May.

At St. Mary's Orphanage on the beach, the nuns gathered their charges—ninety-three terrified boys and girls—and led them in singing spirited hymns to calm their terror. The force of the hurricane winds and water smashed the building. Only three children survived.

A house on North Avenue after the Galveston hurricane.
LIBRARY OF CONGRESS, PRINTS AND PHOTOGRAPHS DIVISION, LC-USZ62-56437

The Littlejohn family fared better. They survived, as did their house on the western side of the isle. Their only loss was a 15-foot climbing jacaranda vine on the side of their house; the salt water that swept through the first floor killed the plant. For the Littlejohns and the other Galvestonians who made it through that terrible Saturday night, Sunday morning confirmed their worst fears for the city.

The urban landscape defied recognition. Frame houses had disintegrated and disappeared. Even the sturdier stone and brick buildings along the Strand—the heart of the city's business district—had been swept away or stood only as gutted shells. At least 6,000 people had died, by some estimates twice that number. Thousands more had serious injuries from flying debris.

While Galvestonians set to work hauling off the dead, the mayor dispatched six men to take the *Phoebe,* one of the very few boats not wrecked in the storm, and get help from the outside world as quickly as possible. The delegation waded ashore at Texas City, hurried to nearby La Marque, and eventually reached Houston. There, at 3 A.M. on Monday, one of them sent a telegram to Texas governor Joseph D. Sayers as well as President William McKinley: "I have been deputized by the mayor to inform you that the city of Galveston is in ruins."

At first, crews of men in Galveston attempted to identify the dead and take them to churches or funeral homes. The task quickly became impossible. Most of the human bodies had been stripped of clothing and mutilated by the force of the storm. Animal carcasses littered the streets as well.

The weather allowed little time for identification or for mourning. In Galveston's subtropic temperatures, corpses decomposed quickly, creating an unbearable stench and the potential for widespread infection. Removing the dead became so distasteful that men with guns were required to keep crews working.

Someone thought of loading bodies onto barges and hauling them 18 miles out into the Gulf, but the waters refused the offerings and washed the storm victims back to shore. Then corpses were stacked in funeral pyres and set ablaze. Even so, the work went slowly.

Floating wreckage near Texas City—a typical scene for miles along the shore.
LIBRARY OF CONGRESS, PRINTS & PHOTOGRAPHS DIVISION, LC-USZ62-122502

Rumors of looting began almost as quickly as the storm abated, but they may have been exaggerated. It was hard to be sure whether someone was looting or trying to identify a loved one by searching for rings or brooches.

One of those searchers, Isaac Cline, hunted everywhere for Cora May. He prayed desperately that she had somehow been spared when their home collapsed.

On Sunday night Thomas McGown began another missive to his brother George.

This has been a terrible day in Galveston. I hope I will never
see another one like it. I have been wading [in] water digging
for dead people all day since 5 o'clock this morning, and it
will take weeks to clear the wreck[age] and . . . a great many
will never be found.

. . . I climbed the debris [on the beach] and looked over.
The gulf was still high . . . and for blocks and miles where
the buildings had stood, there was nothing; and such a pile
of broken buildings and lumber! It is three miles long, 200
feet wide and about 20 feet high, and all through that are
dead people.

He ended his letter with the opinion that "the city of Galveston is a thing of the past. . . . [I]t will never be rebuilt, and will
never recover from the terrible disaster."

McGown underestimated Galveston's determination to
survive.

The offices of the *Daily News* escaped relatively intact, and
Sunday morning's edition listed the names of known dead.
The list grew daily as additional bodies were discovered and
identified.

Help began pouring in as fast as rescue and aid workers
could reach Houston. Clara Barton, founder of the American
Red Cross, was one of the first to respond. Although she was
seventy-eight years old and recovering from *la grippe,* Barton
had valuable experience in disaster relief and went right to
work. She had expected to find many orphans. Instead she
found whole families among the dead. She soon telegraphed
Washington with her assessment: "Situation not exaggerated."
Indeed, the storm was (and remains) the worst disaster in
American history in terms of lives lost, surpassing even Hurricane Katrina.

A man, woman, and children rummage through rubble of destroyed houses following the violent 1900 hurricane that devastated most of Galveston.
LIBRARY OF CONGRESS, PRINTS & PHOTOGRAPHS DIVISION, LC-USZ62-120389

Philanthropists sent trainloads of medical supplies, food, and clothing. The army, which had three coastal artillery forts on the island or in the vicinity that had taken a battering, sent men and equipment. Volunteer work crews came in with saws, hammers, and nails. But not everyone came to help. Newspapers from across the state and nation sent reporters and photographers to the scene. Angry survivors resented the journalistic intruders and smashed cameras when they could.

At least 6,000 died in the storm.
LIBRARY OF CONGRESS, PRINTS & PHOTOGRAPHS DIVISION, LC-USZ62-120937

As many arrived, others departed the devastated island. Steamships carried surviving women and children to the mainland if they had families to receive them.

Isaac Cline continued to search for Cora May among the survivors and the dead. On September 30, more than three weeks after the hurricane, workmen uncovered the body of a woman. Cline was able to recognize Cora May by her wedding ring, and he finally buried her and his unborn child.

The meteorologist had lost his wife, but at least he had been able to identify her. Many family members were not so fortunate. Anywhere from seventy to one hundred corpses were uncovered and burned in a single day, and not until November did the last funeral fires finally die out.

Donations for the people of the stricken city exceeded $1.25 million and came from around the country. Meanwhile, the city government set about restoring utilities and removing debris. Business and home owners repaired office buildings and houses.

As the island rebuilt, a troublesome question persisted: What about next time? That there would be a next time was certain. Galveston Island had been buffeted by storms for as long as anyone remembered.

Engineers planned a 3-mile-long seawall along the eastern edge of the city and down the beach on the Gulf side. The outer side of the wall was concave to carry the force of storm waves up and out. With periodic extensions, the seawall eventually stretched 10 miles down the island, guarding its more populated areas.

But the seawall (which would prove effective in a major hurricane fifteen years later) was only part of the solution. Galveston lay no more than 8.7 feet above sea level. The 1900 storm surge carried almost 16 feet of water across the island.

Engineers came up with an untested plan: Raise the city.

Covering a few square city blocks at a time, workmen jacked up 2,000 buildings—including the ornate St. Patrick's Church—and forced sand beneath them. This was the most extensive public-works project in the state's history to that point,

*Horse-drawn carts for food delivery, protected by armed
guards, outside the Commissary in Galveston.*
LIBRARY OF CONGRESS, PRINTS & PHOTOGRAPHS DIVISION, LC-USZ62-123883

and it proceeded slowly. Some homeowners who lived in the
large, multistory houses that lined Galveston's boulevards simply relocated their parlors and living spaces to the second floor,
while their previous main floors became underground rooms.

As cleanup and relief work continued, city leaders decided that the time had come for a change in Galveston's city government. The financial and commercial leaders of the city opted for a commission form of government. Each commissioner would administer a division of city government: finance and revenue, police and fire, waterworks and sewage, or streets and public improvements. This arrangement worked so well that Galveston kept it until 1960, when it switched to a council-manager system.

While Galveston coped with cleaning and rebuilding, on January 10, 1901, the Lucas geyser in the Spindletop field blew a stream of oil 100 feet into the air. Nearby Beaumont became a boomtown overnight. Houston became the natural choice for corporate petroleum offices and for shipping. Galveston would never regain its position of prominence, nor its title as the "New York City of Texas."

But it did endure. Today Galveston is a popular vacation and convention center. Tours of its elegant Victorian homes and the historic buildings along the Strand celebrate the city of 1900, the year it changed forever.

"GOD SEEMED NIGH"

Goliad Tornado

1902

Early risers in and around Goliad awakened to a gray sky that Sunday morning, but in a rural area largely dependent on agriculture, few people minded the prospect of a rainy day.

One of the oldest towns in the state, the South Texas community traced its roots to Mission Espiritu Santo and the presidio that guarded it against Indians, two stone complexes built by the Spanish on opposite sides of the San Antonio River in 1749. Named Goliad in 1829, the town had seen the massacre of Colonel James Fannin and 341 of his soldiers during Texas's bloody war for independence from Mexico in 1836.

But Texas and Goliad had long since settled into a peaceful routine. The arrival of rail service in 1889 brought increased prosperity. Now, on March 18, 1902, the people of Goliad went about their Sunday activities. Churchgoers returned from services and started frying chickens in preparation for what typically constituted the biggest meal of the week—a noon feast Texans tended to call Sunday dinner. Meanwhile, a hard wind came up from the southeast, gusting to 40 mph. The sun broke through for a while during the noon hour, but that did not last long. By 2:30 P.M., as some folks enjoyed a post-dinner nap, the sky to the northwest of town began turning dark.

Not everyone had time to take it easy, even on a Sunday afternoon. Outside town was a rancher who had driven cattle to market in Kansas in the days before South Texas had rail service. He looked up at the sky. As he watched, small, whirling cones dipped from the clouds. He had never seen that happen before in Goliad County, but he knew what it was: tornadic winds aloft.

The sky darkened and so did the landscape, the giant thunderstorm blocking most of the sunlight. Heavy rain began falling, followed by hailstones bouncing waist-high to anyone unfortunate enough to be outdoors. Alive with lightning, the storm traveled straight toward and then over Goliad; thunder rolled across the county seat as hailstones pelted rooftops.

Around 3:30 P.M. a giant funnel dropped from the clouds south of town, twisting the iron wagon bridge that carried San Patricio Street across the San Antonio River into a mass of debris that one newspaper correspondent said looked "as [if] a man [had crumbled] a reed in his hand." Scattering iron beams like twigs, the tornado churned into an area of modest frame houses occupied by the town's African-American community. Ripping the roof from a black Methodist church, it killed almost everyone gathered there for an afternoon event. Then it moved into a neighborhood of more substantial homes.

A few blocks away, J. W. Browne sat on the front porch of the Fannin Hotel, talking with the owner and a couple of friends. Suddenly they heard what sounded like a train. But Browne knew that no train was due at this time of day. The noise, Browne later recalled, "rapidly increased in power and sound until it sounded like a million-ton engine running away."

Still puzzled by the noise, Browne noticed that the light had changed. The world seemed to have turned a dark reddish brown. "God seemed nigh," Browne later declared. Only a few seconds passed, but not until tree limbs and other debris began blowing past the hotel did Browne and his companions fully comprehend that a tornado had touched down.

As the towering black storm bore down on Goliad, Ella Chilton worried about her husband, Louis. One of the town's few doctors, he had ridden 8 miles south of town to Sarco on an emergency call. She could do nothing for him, but she had two children to protect. She decided to take Kate, her eight-year-old daughter, and Warren, her five-year-old son, to the girls' dormitory at nearby Brooks College. The three-story stone building seemed like a much safer place than their frame home. Struggling against the wind to reach the building, young Kate noted with astonishment a small library of books flying horizontally through the air.

Inside the dormitory Mrs. Chilton, her children, and three other women held each other's hands for both safety and comfort. As they opened a closet door at the bottom of the staircase, the tornado swept over the building, peeling the roof from the building and collapsing a wall. More fascinated than terrified, Kate watched everything from pots and pans to dressers and beds swirling in the air around her until suddenly she, too, became airborne.

"How high I don't know," she would recall, "but high enough to have a quick look at the destruction going on."

The next thing she remembered was rolling in water in the yard outside the wreckage of the dormitory. Bleeding from a

scalp wound, she walked back to the ruins of the college building in search of her mother and brother. Partially buried under
debris, Mrs. Chilton had a broken pelvis, but little Warren had
only some bruises. Two of the other three women who had
taken refuge in the building lay dead nearby.

Northwest of town, fifteen-year-old Gertrude Todd saw
something in the air not far from Goliad. Her family concluded that a horse had been sucked up by the wind. After the
storm passed the Todds went to where the object had fallen.
Instead of an animal carcass, they found a dead woman.

With winds later estimated as strong as 300 mph, the tornado roared across the western half of town, killing people and
animals and turning houses into "avalanches of splinters." In
some instances, as one survivor later put it, the storm also
"reversed the laws of nature." A corncob, transformed by the
ferocious wind into a high-velocity projectile, penetrated a live
oak tree. Stunned chickens wandered around minus all their
feathers but otherwise unharmed. Some residents even said
that when the tornado crossed the San Antonio River, it parted
the water as God had done with the Red Sea in Biblical times.
It all happened in four minutes.

When the cyclone had passed, Browne and his friends
sprinted from the hotel to the area 2 blocks west of the courthouse square where the tornado had struck. Ancient live oaks
had been torn from the ground like weeds, and almost every
structure had been reduced to piles of broken lumber. Browne
saw people lying dead, dying, or bleeding from less severe
injuries.

"Shrieks of the wounded met the ear," Browne told a
reporter for the *Victoria Advocate* a short time later. "The streets
were a litter of dead . . . people, cows, dogs, cats, chickens. In

company with many others, I helped all I could. The dead were on every side, white and black locked in a last death clasp to what they had seized upon."

The office of the town's weekly newspaper, the *Goliad Guard,* escaped destruction. But publisher R. T. Davis's stone house had been heavily damaged. The newspaper's hastily prepared next edition described the catastrophe:

> A space 350 yards wide and a mile long, the western slope of the city, that a few moments before had been covered with pretty homes, handsome flower gardens and orchards; its streets shaded by beautiful trees, many of them giant live oaks that had withstood storms for centuries—was now a wide waste from whose gruesome ruins came the shrieks of the wounded and the dying.
>
> Men rushed together in pairs and small parties, excitedly calling to each other; ran rapidly from one ruin to another, lifting the wounded from under the timbers, laying them down and rushing on to the next cry. 'Twas all they could do just then.

The tornado left nothing the same. An area a mile long and a half mile wide had been, as the local newspaper continued, "swept as with a broom in the hands of some crazed monster demon. Only splinters and fragments were strewn around." Four churches and more than a hundred houses had been destroyed.

Though the tornado had savaged the residential part of town, the telegraph and telephone connections between Goliad and the outside remained intact. At the train station the telegrapher tapped out a quick message: "Terrible cyclone at Goliad

. . . Fifty houses swept away . . . Many people killed." Word of the disaster reached Victoria first, about twenty-five minutes after the storm. "As soon as the news was flashed over the wires on Sunday afternoon," the *Victoria Advocate* reported later that week, "every doctor who could be spared at once made preparations to start for the scene of the disaster. In addition, a large number of citizens volunteered to go and act as nurses."

A special relief train from Victoria reached Goliad at 7 P.M., followed by two more trains later that night. While five doctors and volunteer nurses tended to the injured, members of the O'Connor Guards, a state militia company from Victoria, protected against looting and held back throngs of onlookers. On later trains volunteers came to assist with another vital matter: burying the dead.

Goliad had no hospital, but the undamaged new courthouse quickly became the de facto medical center. A physician from nearby Cuero, Dr. J. H. Reuss, took charge of emergency medical care. "There are forty seriously injured," the *San Antonio Express* soon told its readers. "Possibly 75 percent will recover. . . . Many of the injured will undoubtedly die tonight."

Indeed, doctors treated horrific injuries. "The scenes around the temporary hospitals are heartrending," the *Houston Post* reported, "old men and little children, side by side, the former bereft of families and the latter orphaned, and all suffering excruciating agony." A little girl had to have both of her legs amputated. A young mother had suffered a broken arm, hip, and legs. Volunteers carried a man with a fractured skull to the courthouse. One victim had been impaled by a large piece of lumber. The only thing that could be done for him was to saw off the ends to make it easier for him to be buried.

The county sheriff and county judge did what they could to coordinate rescue efforts, but with 10 percent of the town's residents dead and 20 percent injured, chaos reigned. The absence of any form of city government added to the problem. The people of Goliad had voted to dissolve their community's incorporation in 1896, but at a town meeting on the day after the tornado, the citizenry organized a series of committees that would serve in an ad-hoc capacity. These included a medical committee, a finance committee, a food and assistance committee, and an appeals committee. "Everything now is system," the *San Antonio Express* related a few days later. The day after the tornado, the appeals committee released this statement to the newspapers and had it circulated on handbills printed on the *Advance's* job press:

> To the Public: On the 18th day of May the town . . . was visited with a cyclone which, in its effects, was more horrible than the massacre of Fannin and his command. The prisoners had a certain and speedy death. Not so with all in the storm-swept district, which is a bare waste. . . . Many died after the most acute suffering. . . . Most all of the survivors are absolutely homeless and penniless.
>
> The citizens of Goliad are accepting visitation with brave hearts and giving cheerfully of their portion. Should it be the desire of the State at large to contribute towards a mitigation of our lot subscriptions will be received and acknowledged by the committee.

With memories of the 1900 Galveston storm still fresh on his mind, Governor Joseph D. Sayers wired an urgent appeal from Austin to the mayor of every Texas city with a population

As communicated by a Goliad telegrapher, "Terrible cyclone at Goliad . . .
Fifty houses swept away . . . Many people killed." This 1902 photo says it all.
COURTESY OF GOLIAD COUNTY HISTORICAL COMMISSION

of 3,000 or greater: "Please collect and send as rapidly as possible to county judge of Goliad supplies, food and clothing for
relief of cyclone sufferers."

Residents of Victoria already had taken up a collection for
their stricken neighbors. Later that Monday Goliad County
Judge J. C. Burns signed a receipt for $1,111.75 from the people
of Victoria. Eventually, thanks to the governor's request and
national newspaper coverage, Goliad received more than
$14,000 in cash in addition to donations of goods and services.
Money came from cities as distant as St. Louis and New
Orleans, with the local relief committee parceling out funds
to homeowners who demonstrated that they intended to
rebuild.

Local merchants, some of them having lost homes or family members, opened their stores and "dispensed everything needed for any purpose without cost," as the *Houston Post* noted. Goliad also got corporate help. "Had it not been for the prompt service of the railroad officials," the *Victoria Advocate* reported later that week, "the relief of the Goliad sufferers would have been slow, uncertain and wholly inadequate." The newspaper noted that rail lines sent special trains to the stricken community, allowing nearly a thousand people to ride free. Nor did the railroad charge for carrying any of the supplies sent to Goliad.

Jim Crow was alive and well in Texas and the rest of the South in 1902, but the tornado united the county for at least a little while. "Doctors and nurses have worked heroically and so has everyone, residents and visitors, white and black alike," the *San Antonio Express* said. Even so, the makeshift hospital in the courthouse was for whites only. Not until five days after the storm did anyone get around to setting up a hospital for blacks.

In the days following the tornado, as the San Antonio newspaper put it, "The courthouse was indeed a busy scene, each ward or [department] had its work and did it. . . . To look in upon the different [departments] made one feel the workers knew their business and were doing it." Only four days after the storm, the Goliad County commissioner's court listened to a proposal for rebuilding the San Patricio Street bridge.

A year later the bridge and most of the devastated area had been rebuilt. The county had exempted homeowners in what it referred to as the "Cyclone District" from paying property taxes for those twelve months. Most of the injured had recovered, including Mrs. Chilton, whose husband had escaped injury that afternoon and returned to join his out-of-town colleagues in treating the wounded.

Despite the number of fatalities and the extent of the devastation, the storm soon was forgotten by all but those who had lost family members or friends. Twenty years after the tornado, the Goliad newspaper reprinted some of its 1902 coverage, but on the fiftieth anniversary, there was no mention of the disaster at all.

The National Weather Service attributed 114 deaths to the tornado, but later research by Dr. Karen Fritz, a history professor at Victoria College, revealed the names of 102 victims. Beyond that, records indicate that thirty-four unidentified African-American storm victims lie buried in Goliad's Lott Cemetery. That would make the death toll at least 136, elevating the storm to the deadliest tornado in Texas history.

In 1965 tornado survivor W. L. Lutenbacher, then seventy-seven years old, told the *Houston Chronicle* that he believed the disaster may have claimed as many as 385 lives. "It took so long getting the names," he said. "Some of them we never did know who they were."

Seventy-six years after the event, the Texas State Historical Commission approved a metal historical marker on the tornado for the courthouse square. But on private property elsewhere in town is a more striking, if lesser known, reminder of the storm: a rusty iron beam from the San Patricio Street bridge still imbedded deep in the ground, carried for nearly a mile by killer winds that terrible Sunday afternoon.

THE END OF THE LINE

Locomotive 704 Explosion

1912

P. A. Auen had a good job, but he earned every penny of his pay. With only Sunday off, he worked a regular forty-eight-hour week at the Southern Pacific rail yard, clocking a lot of overtime on top of that.

Since February 21 he had been spending most of his time on Number 704, a one-hundred-ton steam locomotive. Only a few years out of the factory at Philadelphia's Baldwin Locomotive Works, the ten-wheel giant pulled passenger cars along the Galveston, Harrisburg, and San Antonio Railroad, a leg of the Southern Pacific. Damaged in a train wreck at nearby Seguin on December 18, 1911, Number 704 had been undergoing repairs at the SP's Southern Division roundhouse at Tenth and Austin Streets, on the east side of downtown San Antonio.

Just as Auen started to walk out the door on Monday morning, March 18, 1912, his wife threw her arms around his neck and pleaded with him to stay home for the day. But Number 704 was ready to return to service, and Auen wanted to give it a final test. The San Antonio trainmaster had it scheduled for a run that evening.

"Why, that's not buying food and clothing for you and the baby," Auen joked with her, both pleased and annoyed with her request that he stay home.

"I know it," she said, "but do me this one favor this one time. I feel that you ought to stay home today."

Surprised at her persistence, Auen thought it over. Others at the yard were just as capable of checking out the engine as he was. When his wife continued to insist that he stay, he made her a deal. If she would go to the store down the street and buy him the fixings for a good breakfast and a magazine to read, he would stay home.

Auen would not be the only SP employee staying home that day, but the others had a more serious reason. Labor issues had led to a walkout at the busy shop in the fall of 1911. With the majority of its regular boiler repairmen, copper fitters, and other machinists off the job, the railroad had brought in replacement workers from the Midwest and Northeast. Some of these men had yet to collect their first paycheck, several had not even had their names added to the payroll, and some, fearing union reprisal, worked under assumed names. Feelings ran strong, so much so that James Valentine, the assistant roundhouse foreman, carried a pistol.

Longtime engineer Walter Jourdan had grown tired of the whole business and so had his wife, who had been urging him to retire. Jourdan promised her that it would not be long before he hung up his engineer's cap for good. But until then, he still had a job to do.

Number 704 had been tested the day before and seemed to be working fine. But this morning Jourdan did not like what he saw on the pressure gauge as the engine built up steam. He had the boiler fire banked to allow the pressure to drop so he could make a few adjustments.

Now satisfied that the locomotive was back in top operating order, the sixty-three-year-old engineer shouted a simple order: "Warm 'er up."

As a brawny fireman reignited the coal in the firebox, Jourdan moved around the engine, checking fittings and adding a little oil here and there. It would not take long to have a head of steam up. Then the engine could be backed out of the roundhouse and into the yard to be connected to the passenger and baggage cars it would pull that afternoon.

While Jourdan continued to tinker with the massive locomotive, shop painter Jose E. Fuentes dipped his brush into a paint can, putting the finishing touches on the star on the side of the engine's driving rod. Machinist's helper Robert Mantiel stood by the big engine, the centerline of its boiler nearly 6 feet above the track line. Henry C. Mansker Sr., foreman of the blacksmith's shop, talked with his son, James, a machinist. P. J. Stoudt worked in the copper shop, while Archie Price, a pipe fitter, went about his duties. Elsewhere in the large brick building, dozens of others had begun their workweek.

By this point Auen had notified the yard that he would not be coming in that day. As his wife cooked breakfast, he settled down to read the magazine that she had brought him.

Number 704, partially out of the half-moon-shaped roundhouse, idled on the track prior to being backed into the yard. The giant locomotive seemed to be working fine. Above its swinging pendulum, the clock in the roundhouse read 8:55 A.M.

At that instant steam pressurized at more than 200 pounds per square inch, all capitalized on a small crack that had developed in the iron plating that held it in check. The boiler ruptured, launching the huge cylinder through the roundhouse roof like a rocket lying on its side, breaking the big wheels from their hubs, and sending assorted pieces of iron, levers, pipes, rods, and other shrapnel-like hunks of metal in every direction at deadly velocity.

His house shaken to its foundation by the tremendous explosion, Auen realized immediately what had happened. Forgetting his magazine, he ran out of the house, barely aware of his wife's screams.

Those of his coworkers not torn apart by the barrage of flying metal had been scalded by live steam. Instantaneously, a shock wave spread outward, an ever-widening spiral of death and destruction. The southwest portion of the roundhouse disappeared in an explosion of metal, lumber, and bricks.

Expanding farther, the shock wave shot jagged metal fragments, splintered lumber, and now human body parts to the surrounding residential area. The force of the explosion pulled trees from the ground, blew out windows, and rammed debris through the walls of houses a half mile distant. People 20 miles away heard the blast.

The boiler continued to rise until all the steam vented. With its means of propulsion evaporated, the iron began to rain back down on the rail yard and surrounding neighborhood. At 320 Milam Street, Mrs. Ellen Howard had just walked out of her house to check her mail when a waffled piece of iron plate crashed into her home, destroying the back portion of the structure.

Two blocks from the roundhouse, homeowner W. H. Witer heard the explosion and felt the shock wave, followed momentarily by the crash of something hitting his house. When he

The worst railroad boiler disaster in U.S. history was here in San Antonio in 1912. PHOTO FROM THE W. D. HORNADAY COLLECTION, COURTESY OF THE TEXAS STATE LIBRARY AND ARCHIVES COMMISSION

went outside to see what had happened, he found that a human arm had penetrated the tin and lumber of his roof.

Standing in her front yard on Mesquite Street, Mrs. A. P. McCall screamed when someone's torso thudded to the ground. Seconds later an air tank landed right in front of her. At 1217 North Hackberry Street, an iron bolt hit Mrs. August Peters in the head, knocking her unconscious.

Seven blocks from the shattered roundhouse, the front end of Number 704 crashed through the roof of Mrs. B. S. Gillis's house at the corner of Austin and Mason Streets. The impact destroyed the residence and left the sixty-two-year-old woman seriously injured. A small piece of wood an inch square had pierced her hand like a bullet, with another falling object tearing a gash 6 inches long down her leg.

A quarter mile from the scene of the explosion, a 15,000-pound section of engine casing made a crater in the ground. At Hildebrand Brother's Meat Market on North Austin Street, a heavy piece of metal just missed fourteen-year-old John Hildebrand and splintered the store's brand-new icebox.

Between two houses on Duval Street, a huge chunk of locomotive dug 4 feet into the ground where moments before several children had been shooting marbles. A mother's call to breakfast had saved their lives. At 115 Duval the locomotive's steam dome wrecked part of Mrs. E. O. Stephens's house, injuring her.

The shock wave continued to expand from its source, its power lessening with the growing distance. Still, houses and buildings in every part of the city shook from the force of the explosion. Not knowing what had happened, people poured into the streets. Some residents thought San Antonio had experienced an earthquake.

Devastating as the explosion was, many railroad workers survived. Stoudt had dived under a heavy wooden workbench at the sound of the blast. When the roof caved in, the bench saved his life. A similar circumstance spared copper shop foreman T. A. Williamson, though he had been blown under a workbench by the explosion. He remained buried under debris for thirty minutes. Dazed, shop foreman Robert U. Lipscomb pulled himself to his feet 10 yards from where he had been standing when the boiler blew. Startled to see a hat in his hand, he realized that it belonged to the man he had been talking with only moments before. Now the man lay dead nearby.

Other survivors stood silently in and around the wreckage, stunned by the concussion from the blast and the enormity of the destruction. W. J. Eckert, a strikebreaker from Indianapo-

lis, began urging his fellow workers back to reality. After ordering someone to turn in a fire alarm, he organized the first rescue efforts. "To . . . Eckert . . . belongs the credit of bringing
order out of chaos immediately following the explosion," the
San Antonio Light reported the next day.

A huge black cloud billowing skyward revealed the general
location of the explosion. All available firemen and police officers
rushed to the scene. Shortly after word of the enormity of the disaster reached the officer of the day at Fort Sam Houston, a squad
of the Third Cavalry galloped through the city streets to help
overwhelmed city officers and county sheriff's deputies preserve
order. The army also sent medical corpsmen and ambulances.

Emergency workers, family members of those who worked
at the railroad yard, and the general public soon found an
incredible scene of devastation. The southwest side of the
roundhouse had been blown out, as well as the north and
south walls of the machine and blacksmith shops. The roofs of
the structures had collapsed. Everything—man and machinery—within 100 feet of the locomotive had been demolished.
For yards beyond that lay a field of twisted debris.

"The engine . . . was reduced to a scrap heap," the San
Antonio Light reported. "Only a wheel and a few pieces of
twisted iron remained to show that it had been a locomotive."

Though the exploding boiler had caused most of the damage, the energy of the escaping steam had tossed an oil ten-
der—a fuel car attached to the rear of the locomotive—nearly
150 feet, spraying fuel oil over a wide area. The oil soon caught
fire, burning alive some of the railroad workers who had survived the initial blast.

Law enforcement officers, firemen, railroad workers, soldiers, and volunteers worked to pull the injured and dead from

the debris. Everyone who had been in or near the roundhouse had been drenched in the thick, black oil. Embedded fragments of coal and wood made exposed skin, as one San Antonio newspaper reporter put it, "dark as night."

Six doctors who had hurried to the rail yard did what they could for the injured, while horse-drawn ambulances took victims to Santa Rosa Infirmary, the city's largest hospital.

As the recovery effort continued, a broken whistle on one of three damaged locomotives blew deeply at a steadily decreasing decibel level until the engine's boiler pressure finally dropped to zero. "For over two hours," the *San Antonio Light* reported, "the whistle kept up its monotone, like the sigh of some dying soul escaping from the tumultuous scenes of the day."

In addition to the grim work under way at the epicenter of the blast, two-man teams spread out over the neighborhood with a particularly grisly assignment: collecting body parts strewn across the area by the force of the explosion. Carrying baskets covered with white cloth, the teams picked up biological material from the streets and removed remains from trees, utility lines, and rooftops.

Later in the day the San Antonio Traction Company began running extra streetcars to the vicinity of the explosion. An estimated 50,000 people, half of the city's population, came to the area. Brooking no nonsense, Southern Pacific Railroad police and city officers held back curious citizens, blackjacking anyone caught trying to walk off with a piece of debris as a souvenir. The railroad bulls even roughed up a couple of photographers on the staff of the *San Antonio Express*.

The explosion and the oil fire that followed had been devastating. Authorities identified twenty-six bodies, with the remaining accumulation of body parts and viscera suggesting that at least another ten to fifteen men had died in the blast. An additional fifty people, railroad employees and neighborhood residents, suffered injuries.

Even as railroad workers and others continued to clear debris, railroad and local officials put together a board of inquiry to determine the cause of the tragedy. The fourteen-member committee had no legal standing, but the following day it met for more than five hours and inspected the disaster scene.

The chairman of the Texas Railroad Commission, Allison Mayfield, and Commissioner William Williams arrived in San Antonio the same day and conferred with Southern Pacific officials. Mayfield told local newspaper reporters that he had wired the chairman of the federal Interstate Commerce Commission to request an ICC investigation of the explosion.

Two ICC boiler inspectors reached San Antonio on March 21, and the official board of inquiry—made up of Railroad Commission officials, SP officials, and representatives of the Texas attorney general's office—began taking testimony the next day.

The railroad also requested that the Texas Labor Statistics Commission look at the incident. After inspecting the disaster scene and talking with witnesses, Commissioner J. A. Starling told the *San Antonio Express:* "Speaking from forty years experience in this line of work, I am convinced beyond doubt that the occurrence was caused by tremendous boiler pressure. . . . Of course there is no telling just what the pressure was, as the steam gauge was wrecked, or whether there was the proper supply of water, but there is no question that the boiler pressure was responsible for this terrible accident."

As the explosion readily demonstrated, working for the railroad was a dangerous way to make a living. Nationwide from 1890 to 1917, railroad companies lost 72,000 employees in work-related accidents. Additionally, 158,000 railroad workers died in roundhouse and repair-shop accidents. Steam boilers posed a particularly high level of danger. Though accidents were common, the San Antonio explosion remained the nation's deadliest railroad boiler disaster for the remainder of the steam locomotive era.

Given the tense atmosphere of the strike, immediate suspicion arose that the tragedy might have been an act of labor violence.

"At first, people suspected strikers of sabotaging the locomotive out of fear of losing their jobs to the strikebreakers," John Kight recalled years later. "But after a thorough investigation, engineers ruled out dynamite or any other exterior cause."

Even so, no one ever determined the exact cause of the disaster. Everything pointed to the failure of the steam engine's safety valve, but whether the problem was mechanical or the result of human error remains a mystery.

Though the explosion stands as the Alamo City's worst man-made disaster, it has been virtually forgotten. But John Hildebrand never forgot his experience that March morning in his family's meat market near the SP yard. For the rest of his long life, Hildebrand kept an L-shaped fragment from Number 704's bell as a reminder of how close he came to dying young.

FIRE STRIKES TWICE

Paris Goes Up in Flames
1916

John (Mutt) Cross had the day off on Tuesday, March 21, 1916. Tall and heavyset, the twenty-year-old straddled his Indian motorcycle and rode to his girlfriend's house about a mile from downtown Paris, a thriving Texas city about 100 miles northeast of Dallas. As the couple discussed their plans for the evening, Cross heard the clanging of the fire bell back at the Central Station.

Looking out the door, the young fireman saw black smoke rolling into the sky from the city's warehouse district. Realizing that it must be a pretty bad fire, Cross figured he had better get back to the station.

Alternating his attention between the growing plume of smoke and the road, Cross raced his motorcycle back downtown. But by the time he got to the station, all the equipment had already rolled out the doors. Cross grabbed his coat and helmet and waved down a passing motorist to hitch a ride toward the smoke.

The Paris Fire Department had been in a transitional phase for several years, as were most of the nation's departments. For decades horse-drawn fire wagons had been the mainstay of firefighting. The old, reliable equipment still had its place in Paris, but the city also had a few motorized pumpers. Stout enough to easily crank the motor to life, Cross had been named driver of the one of the new gasoline-powered fire engines.

Firemen did not receive much, if any, formal training, but they learned by experience. When Cross reached the source of the smoke, a one-story frame warehouse at Frisco Avenue and Fourth Street Southwest near the railroad tracks, he knew that he would not be getting back to his girlfriend's house any time soon. Energized by a stiff southwest wind that had been blowing all day, the fire absorbed the streams of water shooting toward it with no noticeable effect. Cross knew that if he and his colleagues did not get the blaze knocked down in a hurry, the wind-driven flames would spread to other buildings.

Finding his truck, Cross took charge of the pumper and crew. Just as he had feared, wind gusting at more than 40 mph blew embers toward a residential area north of Frisco Avenue. Homeowners desperately tried to protect their property with garden hoses and water buckets, but fires soon began popping up on shingled roofs. Putting any more water on the warehouse would be useless. Now the firemen had houses to save.

Cross had his men bring in their line so that he could drive the truck around between the flaming warehouse and the residential area. Hooking their hose to another hydrant, the firemen soon had several hundred feet out. As Cross checked the pressure on the pumper, the smoke got so thick that he could no longer see the other firefighters. Around the same time he felt the temperature rising. Seconds later, wind-driven flames licked around the truck.

Trapped, Cross jerked an ax off the truck and swung it down on the charged line. Water exploded from the severed hose, dousing Cross and the truck in a cooling spray that saved his life and the pumper. Though he was no longer in immediate danger, he realized the blowing flames still cut him off from the other firemen. Elsewhere in town, word spread that Cross had died in the fire.

Working alone in his downtown law office, former Texas chief justice W. F. Moore answered the telephone on his desk. His wife wanted to know if he knew what was burning. Moore had not heard about the fire, but he understood immediately the danger posed by the wind. A deliberate man, he got up from his desk, locked his papers in the firm's safe, and walked downstairs to see what was going on. Just as he walked outside, he saw a burning shingle drifting through the air. It landed on the roof of the building immediately across from his Lamar Avenue office.

"He never went back upstairs," his daughter Margie Lou Hubbard later recalled. "He came straight home and told my mother that there was no way we were going to save the house from being burned."

By 7 P.M. the situation had grown from serious to catastrophic. Fanned by the seemingly incessant wind, the fire continued to spread; the conflagration headed through the city's residential neighborhoods straight for downtown. By telegraph and telephone, Paris mayor Ed H. McCuistion requested help from any fire departments in the area that could get equipment to his town of more than 12,000 residents.

When the fire finally moved past him, Cross again drove his truck toward the smoke. By now the sun had set, but a wide line of fire lit up the sky. From as far as 25 miles away, a flickering orange glow could be seen in the direction of Paris.

A horse-drawn hose wagon and team arrived from nearby Hugo, Oklahoma, by train and was at work by 8:30 P.M. Thirty minutes later a fire truck arrived from Bonham, having made the 38-mile trip in just over an hour. Seven firemen from Honey Grove arrived about the same time. At 9 P.M. a pumper reached the burning city from Cooper, in Delta County.

Hoping they could stop the fire by starving it to death, firefighters and volunteers began using dynamite to destroy homes in its path. But that only produced piles of dry lumber and scattered shingles—more kindling for the raging inferno.

Working desperately, the Moores packed their more important possessions. When they had gathered as much as they could, they took everything to a friend's home on Pine Bluff Street, 6 blocks away. They hoped that firemen would get the blaze under control before it reached their house, but if it did, they figured that the house on Pine Bluff would be spared. Before the evening ended, both residences were destroyed.

The fire continued to move northeast through the city, spreading out like a lady's folding fan. As local and out-of-town firemen battled to stop the firestorm, windblown embers landed on the wood-shingled Gothic roof of the Episcopal church on South Main, near Sherman Street. Located 2 blocks beyond the fire line, the frame church exploded into flames. Now the fire raged on the southern edge of the business district, and the merciless wind continued.

Shortly before 11 P.M. the fire reached the courthouse square, stopping the clock in the courthouse tower one hour before midnight. For the next hour the fire raged in the heart of the city, gutting stores, banks, and other places of business. Finally, the wind died and the fire burned itself out.

The rising sun revealed an incredible scene. Downtown could have passed for the blackened remnants of Civil War Atlanta after Sherman's march. A reporter for a Dallas newspaper likened it to the conflict then raging across the Atlantic: "The scenes in Paris, the once beautiful North Texas city, rival in their piles of wreckage and debris anything that has been seen in war-ridden Europe."

In the central business district, only a few brick and concrete structures remained. One of them was the aptly named Gibraltar Hotel. The newly constructed Belford Apartments and First National Bank, though gutted, also remained structurally sound.

Of the 2,500 acres that lay within the city limits, 270 acres had been charred. At its northern edge the area of destruction stretched a mile across. More than 1,400 structures had been destroyed. Homes, schools, churches, businesses, and government buildings—including the Lamar County courthouse, city hall, the federal building, and the post office—had been leveled or gutted in the conflagration.

Few in town had been able to get any sleep overnight, but no one had time for rest. People began poking through the smoldering ruins of what had been their homes, looking for any possessions that might have endured the flames.

For many old-timers, the fire had been like reliving a nightmare. Thirty-nine years before, on August 31, 1877, fire had destroyed 75 percent of the business district and many residences. Paris had been a smaller town back then, but the blaze consumed most of 14 blocks in the center of the community, covering roughly ten acres. Property-loss estimates ranged from $350,000 to $500,000.

The only thing accidental about that fire had been its extent. About 4 P.M. that day, a saloon owner named Andy Myers had refused his drunken stepson's request for money to continue his binge. The young man, Taylor Pounds, decided to get even with Myers by burning down his business. Unfortunately for Paris, the fire spread beyond the saloon and raced across town. Pounds, meanwhile, sobered up enough to realize that he was in big trouble. He went into hiding, but officers later found him in a weed-covered vacant lot.

Rather than lock Pounds up in the local jail, the officers took him to Bonham to keep him safe from lynching. At a town meeting the next day, several ministers and elected officials addressed the citizenry and convinced them to let the matter proceed through the criminal justice system. A committee then went to Bonham and escorted the prisoner back to Paris. Later tried in Delta County on a change of venue, Pounds was convicted of arson and assessed a four-year prison sentence. But before he could be removed to the penitentiary in Huntsville, he escaped and was never again seen in Paris.

Though the 1877 fire had been a disaster, it paled in comparison to the 1916 fire. Surveying the blackened landscape of what had been one of Texas's major cities, fireman Cross noticed quite a few people digging in their gardens. He thought that was pretty strange until he finally noticed someone brushing dirt from silverware. Seeing other people pulling bulging blankets from the ground, he realized that they had buried their valuables before fleeing the flames that eventually engulfed their homes.

Intending to resume commerce as soon as possible, bankers and other business owners cleared debris from the courthouse square and put up tents. In the case of the financial institutions, bank officers and tellers had to wait until exhausted firemen could hose down their still-hot vaults. The postmaster quickly set up a temporary office and told residents that they could pick up their out-of-town mail directly from the mail cars at Union Depot.

Midday approached on March 22, and the blistered, soot-covered firemen had done all they could. Just as they were about to settle down for a little rest, a report came in that a fire raged out of control in Detroit, a railroad town in adjoining Red River County. Though exhausted, the firemen responded to the alarm. It took them the rest of the day to get it under control.

In Paris that afternoon civic leaders gathered at the Centenary Methodist Church to organize a relief committee. Members collected $20,000 from local residents, with an equal amount coming from elsewhere in Texas in the form of cash or supplies.

"Paris is indebted to a generous and sympathetic public to such an extent that all hope of adequate and detailed acknowledgment has been abandoned," the seven-member committee said in a statement published in the city's two newspapers a few days later. "Our situation is now well in hand," the statement continued, "and unless a protracted spell of bad weather should set in before our housing work is complete, there will be no reason for further concern on our account."

Neither did Paris want an influx of people looking for construction jobs. "Those who are arriving are becoming charges [a burden] almost to as great an extent as those of our own people who suffered actual fire loses," the committee pronounced. The committee went on to warn the rest of Texas and other states that some people "claiming to be refugees

*A photographer with a spring-powered camera recorded this view of the
devastation in downtown Paris the day after the 1916 fire.*
FROM THE AUTHOR'S COLLECTION

from Paris" had been trying to con good-hearted people out of
money.

Money certainly was an issue. Insurance companies paid
Paris residents $5 million in property loss. Owners without
coverage lost at least another $5 million worth of property,
though some estimates were higher. "Guesses at the loss
ranged from seven to fifteen million dollars," longtime *Paris
News* editor A. W. Neville wrote in 1937, "but were guesses pure
and simple." He personally thought that the $8 million figure
was "was probably about correct."

Newspaper ads told the story: "Temporary Quarters J.O.
Pirtle Company Tent on High School lot, Lamar Ave. Men's
work clothes, shoes etc. NO ADVANCE IN PRICE." The
Gibraltar Hotel proclaimed in another ad that it had been fully
protected by fire insurance "and emerges from the fire
unscathed financially and prepared to take care of every obliga-
tion. The Gibraltar will at once repair the fire damage to its
building, adding two additional stories to enable it to properly
take care of the public."

The cause of the fire proved as hard to pin down as its
monetary impact. Some believed that sparks from a railroad

switch engine had ignited dry grass along the right of way. Several lawsuits brought against the railroad advanced this theory, but it did not hold up in court. Others said that a trash fire in a residential yard threw off a burning ember that landed near enough to the warehouse to start the fire. Still others assigned blame to a truck driver who had lit a cigarette and tossed the burning match.

No matter how the fire started, the wind had been the real villain. First it turned a small fire into a big fire. Then it held down and spread the superheated air generated by the fire, pushing a wave of radiant heat ahead of the flames, igniting all structures in its path.

As Neville later concluded, "No fire department could have saved the city unless it had been immediately at hand when the first fire was seen."

In terms of property loss, the Paris fire had been the most disastrous blaze in Texas history and the fifth worst nationally. Only the 1871 Peshtigo (Wisconsin) and Chicago fires, the 1904 Baltimore fire, and the fire that followed the 1906 San Francisco earthquake resulted in greater property damage than the Paris conflagration. The fires in Wisconsin, Illinois, and California claimed many lives, though the Baltimore disaster killed only one person. Miraculously, the death toll in

Paris came to only four, though hundreds lost all their material possessions.

But few seemed to lose their spirit. "The new Paris spirit has manifested itself in such a noble way as to create a wave of enthusiasm among our own people and cause the outside world to look on with genuine admiration," the *Paris Daily Advocate* reported. "Paris of yesterday is not Paris of today, and Paris of today will not be Paris of tomorrow."

DEADLY DROUGHT-BREAKER

Central Texas Flood

1921

The first day it started raining, the people of Central and South Texas took it as good news.

"Central Texas Drouth Ends," the September 9, 1921, edition of the *Austin Statesman* proclaimed in a banner headline. The first paragraph of the page-one story set the scene: "Breaking a drouth that had prevailed for more than two months, drying up small streams and water holes and causing heavy losses to farmers and stockmen, rain . . . began falling throughout Central Texas early this morning."

By noon that Friday the weather station at the University of Texas had measured 1.3 inches of precipitation. That marked the first measurable rainfall in the capital city since July 8, when a little more than three-quarters of an inch had fallen.

Cooling temperatures as well as watering yards and gardens, the wet weather demonstrated the meaning of the old Texas expression "welcome as rain."

"Despite the little inconvenience which the rains caused," the *Statesman* continued, "nobody fretted about it, because it all comes as a pleasant surprise." The surprising nature of the weather event would continue, but the word *pleasant* soon lost its relevance.

The meteorological factors leading to the drought-breaker began on the morning of September 6, when a tropical storm developed in the warm Bay of Campeche. By afternoon the storm had compacted, with towering rain-filled clouds swirling around a small eye. The storm would have become even more powerful had it been farther out in the Gulf of Mexico with more time to spend over warm water, but prevailing wind currents pushed it ashore at the old Mexican port of Veracruz only twenty-four hours after its birth.

After lashing that coastal city, the rain-swollen system followed a northeast course to Texas. Crossing the Rio Grande at Rio Grande City in the lower river valley on the night of September 7, the storm decreased below the level of a tropical depression. But it remained laden with precipitation as it drifted toward the parched, unsuspecting middle of the state.

In San Antonio a light rain began to fall on Thursday, September 8. The rain continued the next day and grew heavier. Lingering over the northern portion of Bexar County, the storm dumped 1.5 feet of rain.

For the people of San Antonio, the rain could not have fallen in a worse place. The northwest part of the county rose higher above sea level than any other area of the county. On top of that, the rocky ground could not absorb much water. The only place that excessive precipitation could go was downhill. Cascading down hillsides and draws, the water collected in Apache and Olmos Creeks and surged from these two streams into the San Antonio River, bearing down on the Alamo City.

The San Antonio River flows through the heart of San Antonio—and its history. Native Americans had been living along the river for millennia by the time the first Europeans arrived in 1691. When members of a Spanish exploring party, or *entrada*, celebrated Mass on the banks of the river on June 13 that year, Franciscan priest Damien Massanet named the stream San Antonio because it happened to be the Feast Day of Saint Anthony. In the 1700s Spain established five missions along the river, harnessing the stream to flow through a 15-mile irrigation network.

Periodically, spring or fall rains sent the river on a rampage. Two of the more severe floods occurred in 1819, when Texas still belonged to Spain, and in 1845, the year the United States annexed it. In between, San Antonio had gone from Spanish to Mexican control, and then, less than two months after the fall of the Alamo on March 6, 1836, it had become the principal settlement of the independent Republic of Texas. After Texas statehood the town continued to grow throughout the nineteenth century and into the twentieth century. In 1921, with 175,000 residents, San Antonio ranked as the state's largest city.

By midafternoon that September 9, the precipitation increased in intensity and continued after sunset. "The electric display was the most vivid ever seen here as lightning flashed almost continuously and the thunder boomed and reverberated," the *San Antonio Express* reported. Even so, the newspaper continued, "The people of San Antonio were caught without warning."

Sudden rises on Alazan and Martinez Creeks sent water ripping through low-lying residential areas on the city's west and south sides. "Rescue workers began helping dwellers of the flooded districts to safety as early as 11 o'clock [P.M.]," the *Express* continued. "At least 500 people owe their lives to police, firemen, soldiers from Fort Sam Houston and Camp Travis, and volunteers who time and again plunged into water shoulder deep . . . to carry women and children to safety."

When water began to rise in the city's residential sections, a neighbor awakened off-duty police traffic officer U. L. Springer, who lived with his wife at 908 Avenue A. Springer and his neighbor left immediately for the nearby residence of an elderly invalid, whom they carried to safety.

Wading back to his house in waist-deep water, the policeman checked his next-door neighbors, who had recently moved to San Antonio. "I placed them in a tree and there the woman and her daughter remained throughout the flood [a period of several hours]," the officer later told a reporter for the *San Antonio Light*. "I did not have time to get them to high ground."

Finally back at his house, Springer found that his wife had helped three women and a child to safety, wading in swirling water that reached her shoulders. Now she and her husband had to save themselves. "Just as . . . we had gotten far beyond the high water," the officer continued, "there appeared a wall of water that swept our house away."

As soon as he could get to police headquarters, Springer reported for official duty wearing a faded blue shirt and cotton pants, his uniforms and everything else he owned lost in the flood. The only items he had managed to hang on to were his badge and gun.

"Entire families were washed away," police motorcycle officer Jack Thompson later told a reporter. "The cries of the helpless and the barking of hundreds of dogs made the night one of terror. We saw people within twenty-five feet of us, yet unable to reach them. One, an old Mexican man, was on a house. We tried to reach him with a rope and would have probably succeeded, but the building collapsed carrying him with it down stream."

People tried to help their fellow residents. "Perhaps the outstanding heroism of the flood," the *Express* reported, "was that of a twelve-year-old Mexican boy who clung to a tree on South Flores Street for five hours, holding on his shoulders above the water a child five years old. The boy rescuer was battered black and blue by floating wreckage and was taken to a hospital conscious. But the child was unharmed."

The twelve-year-old was not the only youthful hero. Sylvia Vanness, fifteen, and her thirteen-year-old brother heard cries for help from the other side of the water rushing down the street in front of their residence. "By the feeble light of a lantern," the Associated Press later reported, "[they] saw two small boys clinging to a tree across the street. The girl and her brother put on bathing suits and attempted to cross."

Finding the water too deep and swift, the teenagers made their way upstream from the tree and jumped in the water, letting the current carry them to the stranded boys. "Between them they carried the two boys back across the street, landing below their home," the wire story continued.

Both boys suffered from exposure, and one of them had been injured by floating debris. That child later died, but the other survived.

By midnight that Friday nearly fifty houses had been washed away, "churned into a shapeless mass of debris," as one San Antonio newspaper put it. Now the flood crest moved toward downtown. As policemen and firefighters watched apprehensively, the river continued to rise. It had flooded before, but never like this.

Market and Navarro Streets after the San Antonio flood.
FROM THE COLLECTION OF CHRIS POWERS

At 1:30 A.M. on Saturday, September 10, a 12-foot wave swept across much of downtown. People still awake raced up stairs in the city's high-rise buildings, barely ahead of the lapping floodwaters. Others, trapped outside, washed downstream in the powerful flood surge.

The floodwaters tore through both of the city's newspaper plants, leaving their giant presses covered with mud. The management of the *Light* made arrangements with the St. Anthony Hotel to use the small job press it had for printing menus; the paper had an extra on the streets by 6 A.M.

"At 5 A.M. Police Commissioner Phil Wright stated that undoubtedly there is a heavy loss of life," the extra reported.

"Water rose almost to the mezzanine floor of the Gunter [Hotel]. . . . [T]here are no electric lights and no power."

Local news writers had much work ahead of them that day, but with first light, the devastation said it all. "This flood is the greatest disaster in the history of San Antonio," the extra continued. "Such structures as the Brady Building, Wolff and Marx Department Store, Stowers, St. Mary's Church and school buildings, the St. Anthony Hotel, the Elks Club . . . several hospitals, the central telephone exchange, the city hall and police and fire headquarters and countless other structures along the low-lying river valley were in the pathway of the flood."

San Antonio had been hit with the most disastrous flood in its long history, but the storm had not finished with Texas. From San Antonio, the precipitation-laden weather system moved northeast, dumping 18.23 inches of rain on Austin, the state capital.

Though downtown Austin lay adjacent to the flood-prone Colorado River, the city escaped any serious flooding. South of town, however, six persons drowned along Onion Creek. Floodwaters also washed away three steel bridges in Travis County.

Just north of Austin, Williamson County took a much more severe blow. The north and south forks of the San Gabriel River went on a rampage. At its juncture with Brushy Creek, the river became 10 miles wide. The Little River also flooded, cresting at 53.2 feet in Cameron, the seat of Milam County. Continuing its northeastern track, the storm left the Brazos River running 54 feet deep at Bryan. Swollen to more than ten times their normal depths, the Little and Brazos Rivers both raged over their banks.

It took a while for the enormity of the disaster to sink in. Floodwaters washed out telephone and telegraph lines, making

Houston Street looking east from San Antonio River Bridge.
FROM THE COLLECTION OF CHRIS POWERS

communication with the rest of the state virtually impossible. Washouts also interrupted railroad service, further hampering the spread of news. Except for the larger urban areas, communities coped in isolation with the flood, not realizing that the disintegrating tropical storm had affected 10,000 square miles of the state. Three days went by before the Associated Press reported that more than 200 people had died in the flood.

With fifty-one deaths and thirteen people missing and presumed dead, San Antonio got most of the headlines, but other areas endured not only a higher death toll but also a more severe fatality rate. Williamson County, population 42,934, lost ninety-three people in the flood; eighty-seven of those victims were in or around the railroad town of Taylor in the eastern half of the county.

The flooding in Williamson County had been along the San Gabriel River and its tributaries, including Brushy Creek.

"One man told of seeing four people floating down Brushy Creek on a huge log," the *Austin Statesman* reported on September 15. "The current was going so swiftly no help could be rendered. Nothing has been heard of them since." Along the same stream six people, including two children, climbed into a tree to escape the rising water. The newspaper continued:

> One of the most pathetic scenes was that of four year old Arnold Jackson and his sister, Texas Jackson, seven years old. The children, together with their uncle, W.D. Barfield, Charlie Cunningham, Mrs. Kelly and Ruby Cunningham, had climbed into a tree for safety. The children after being in the tree for many hours were so overcome by the rain and cold that they lost their hold and fell into the swollen stream below. The other people in the tree remained there thirty-six hours without food. They were finally taken from the tree by a rescuing party.

The death toll went in the record books as 224, but given the racial prejudices of the times, some deaths may have gone unrecorded. Even so, Texas had experienced the deadliest flood in its history, and one of the most damaging. The estimated property loss came to $19 million, with more than a quarter of that in San Antonio. As the Associated Press reported, "Thousands of acres of rich bottom land have been swept clean of crops and many cattle and mules have been drowned."

The storm also set precipitation records. Thrall, a small town in Williamson County between Taylor and the county seat at Georgetown, recorded 38.2 inches of rain in twenty hours. That still stands as the most rainfall ever measured in one day at a U.S. weather station.

Three days after the San Antonio flood, a survivor named
Maude scribbled this note on the back of a hastily marketed
postcard showing damage from the flood:

Dear Folks:
We are safe after water rushing through our street 2 feet
deep. The business part is at a stand still. This is one of the
businesses. Elmer gone[.] All week at washouts. I sure
thought our apartment was flooded but only up to porch.

The storm touched Maude's life and thousands of others,
but the flood of 1921 resulted in the transformation of San
Antonio.

"The press rooms of the rivals [the *Express* and *Light*]
hadn't been pumped dry when each newspaper editorialized
fervently in support of a city-wide network of canals, and the
erection of a detention dam spanning the Olmos Valley to prevent damaging floods," Trinity University history professor
Char Miller later wrote.

Not that the need for flood control was a new issue in the
Alamo City. Earlier that year city officials had seriously discussed covering the river with concrete and transforming it
into a sewer. When news of the plan leaked to the press on
March 31, 1921, San Antonio officials had to deal with a different sort of flood: one of public protest. The idea went on the
shelf, but engineers had warned that a hundred-year flood (an
inundation with a statistical likelihood of occurring once in a
century) could cause tremendous loss of life and property.

The flood that followed six months later amounted to the
worst-case scenario that the engineers had feared. Two years
later, after the election of a new mayor, work began in earnest

to tame the San Antonio River. The 1,900-foot Olmos Dam was completed in 1927, followed two years later by a project called the Great Bend Cut-Off, a flood bypass channel to divert water past the downtown bend in the river. That same year, 1929, architect Robert H. H. Hugman outlined for city leaders a proposal for what he called the "Shops of Romula and Aragon."

The classically rooted name did not catch on, but Hugman's concept did. Starting in 1938, the federal Works Progress Administration began construction of a series of sidewalks, pedestrian bridges, and various parklike features in the heart of the city along the river. The area became known as *Paseo del Rio,* or the River Walk.

Today the River Walk—a stretch of landscaped waterfront with hotels, restaurants, clubs, shopping centers, and other primarily tourist-oriented businesses—winds for 2.5 miles through downtown. Making San Antonio a kind of Southwestern Venice, this area annually funnels nearly $800 million into the city's economy. As such, it remains one upbeat legacy of a killer flood.

"BLOWN AWAY"

Rocksprings Tornado
1927

Herman Fleischer and one of his sons, Gus, worked as mechanics in a family-owned auto garage. They left the shop together on April 12, 1927, and headed to their respective homes for supper. On their way, both men noticed a hard east wind and black clouds building up toward the northwest.

"Clouds had been gathering in the north for an hour or so," J. B. Smith told the *San Angelo Standard* the following day, "but people thought only a possible hailstorm was coming."

Smith, in Rocksprings on business, had a room at the Ballentine Hotel, a two-story building overlooking the Edwards County courthouse. "We had just finished eating supper," he continued. "There were about twenty-five of us, fifteen women. Some had been sitting on the porch, but the wind got so high they had to come in."

Meanwhile, at Claud Gilmer's house, Claud's wife Georgia laid out a suit for him to wear to an 8 P.M. program at the high school. They had just finished their supper and Georgia, then three months pregnant, sat in her favorite rocking chair with their two-year-old daughter in her lap.

Just as Claud went to change clothes for the event, he heard something crash on the porch. Then another crash and another. Flipping on a light, Claud opened the door to identify the source of all that loud noise. As he looked out, a jagged piece of ice as big around as a saucer shattered on the porch. Then another chunk of ice penetrated the roof and ceiling, falling to the floor in the Gilmers' bedroom.

Still standing at the open door, Claud realized the east wind had stopped. For a moment everything seemed to stand still—no motion, no sound. Then he heard a terrible roar, like nothing he had ever heard before, coming from the northwest. Only then did he comprehend that a tornado had dropped from the clouds over the small town.

"I pushed Georgia and our daughter away from the front of the fireplace and hard against the wall," he later told the *San Antonio Express*. "We put our little girl on a wood box, and then both of us leaned over her."

Laced with lightning, rain fell in torrents. "Looking out the west window," Claud said, "in one flash of lightning I saw the Presbyterian church and parsonage. . . . On the next flash they were gone."

Back at the Ballentine Hotel, guests had gathered in the first-floor office at the approach of the storm. "First the roof of the office, which was of frame material, went off, then the upper story and the porch," Smith told the San Angelo newspaper. "We heard things blowing against the house and a terrific roar accompanied by flashes of lightning."

At that, the occupants ran to a newly constructed wing made of concrete and waited out the storm without anyone being injured. "The wind lasted from three to five minutes," Smith said, "but it seemed like hours to us."

"When the wind died down," he continued, "one of the men walked to the lobby and looked out. He came running back yelling 'Boys, let's get out of here. The whole town's been blown away.'"

At his house Gus Fleischer lit a kerosene lantern and set it on a buffet in the dining room when the lights went out. About then the wind sucked out the glass in the bedroom windows, and Gus and his wife, Velma, heard bricks flying off the chimney.

Velma shouted for Gus to get away from the lamp, in case the wind blew it over and spread flaming oil. But Gus could not hear her over the wind.

Though everyone would tell a different story about what happened to them when the storm hit, all of the survivors later agreed on one thing: After the tornado passed, a silence settled over the community that, in its way, seemed as overpowering as the roar of the tornado that had just ripped through town. The rain continued to come down in sheets, but the wind had gone.

The quiet lasted only a minute or so.

By the time Smith emerged from the damaged hotel, he said, "it was bedlam outside. Women screamed at the top of their voices. Moans of the injured. . . . The frantic cries lasted only for a few minutes, then the rescue work began. . . . Everything on the north side of town had been blown down."

Next door to the hotel, the Methodist church and its brand-new parsonage had been leveled, with only the cedar foundation posts remaining. Smith saw the minister, H. L. Spiers, unconscious on the ground. "In a tree only a few feet away was his wife clutching in death her year-old baby, also dead. The tree had been blown down and she had been blown into it," Smith recalled. The pastor later died.

When the wind stopped, the Fleischers had no time to reflect on what had just happened. Neighbors from across the street ran in their front door with incredible news: The tornado had picked up their house, which used to face south, and set it back down, facing west. Other than that, their home suffered little damage.

But the storm had churned right through the heart of the small sheep- and goat-ranching town on the western edge of the Texas Hill Country, destroying or damaging nearly every business and house. Scores lay dead.

As the Fleischers stood on their porch, still trying to comprehend how the storm had reoriented their neighbors' house, someone began pounding on the back door. Mrs. Fleischer rushed to see who it was and found a little girl who said that she did not know where her parents were.

When Gus went into the rain to look for the girl's family, he saw that their house had disintegrated. In a few moments he located the girl's mother, her body jammed against a wooden fence by the force of the wind. At first Gus thought that she was dead, but she was still breathing, though badly hurt.

Carrying the woman inside his house, Gus noticed that her face was black. It took him a moment to figure it out: The tornado had injected flying dirt into the pores of her exposed skin.

Gus realized that Rocksprings had taken a catastrophic blow. He got into his car to go see how his father and mother had fared. Driving toward their garage, Gus saw that most of the buildings around the courthouse square had been destroyed or heavily damaged. The courthouse had lost its roof, but its rock walls still stood. Gilmer's drugstore had been torn from its foundation, as had the building used by the Rocksprings Telephone Company. But the company's small switchboard and the evening telephone operator, Mrs. Gladys Laurie, had survived the storm.

Seeing the flicker of a small light, Laurie crawled through the wreckage toward the switchboard. Thanks to a battery, the equipment still worked. Laurie inserted a plug into the Kerrville line and put on her earphones, hoping to alert the operator on the other end that Rocksprings had been devastated. For a moment she heard the operator's faint voice, but before she could say anything, the line went dead.

In a different part of town, telephone lineman Foster Owens emerged from beneath a battered table under which he and his wife and children had ridden out the storm. Telling his wife that he had to get help, Owens left his house and made his way through twisted corrugated roofing, splintered wood, and fallen trees to the now-nonexistent telephone company office.

Shining a light on the debris, Owens found Laurie. She told him that the lines were dead and probably down. Owens remembered that he had a telephone in his truck—the test set he used in the field when repairing line. With Laurie at the wheel of her undamaged Model T, they drove around the wreckage, heading east of town on the road to Kerrville.

About a mile down the gravel road, Owens saw that the telephone wires were still up. Laurie stopped the car, and the lineman climbed the nearest pole to splice into the wire.

A hundred miles to the east, an operator in Kerrville plugged into a ringing long-distance circuit. Rocksprings had been devastated by a cyclone, Owens yelled into the portable phone. The town badly needed help.

That message delivered, Owens extended some wire to the ground so that Laurie could use his headset to stay in communication with the outside world. With the rain still falling and

The view from the top of the courthouse showed the extent of the
damage in Rocksprings.   COURTESY ROCKSPRINGS HOTEL

lightning crashing, Laurie remained at the makeshift communication center all night, relaying messages of grief and hope
as she received them.

Later that evening she told an operator in San Antonio that
she believed as many as 126 people had been killed by the
storm. After asking her Alamo City counterpart to spread the
word that more help was needed, Laurie broke the connection.
She had others to call.

Based on the first call to San Antonio, the Army Signal
Corps's Kelly Field radio facility notified the on-duty signal officer at Fort Clark, a cavalry post about 50 miles south of Rocksprings in Kinney County. By 11 P.M., only three hours after the
killer twister roared through Rocksprings, a contingent of cavalry had saddled up and ridden to the relief of the stricken town.

Amanda Eastland, a Rocksprings schoolteacher, had been
among the diners at the Ballentine Hotel when the storm

struck. Commandeering an automobile, she drove 20 miles toward her native Sonora until she reached the Ruby Davis Ranch and a working telephone. From there she called Sonora to report the tornado and its consequences.

Meanwhile, tragedy compounded tragedy. The town's water tower, weakened by the tornado, collapsed in a pile of twisted metal. The tank ruptured, releasing 50,000 gallons of water and drowning several victims still prostrate from the storm.

Among the dead was Ripley Dollohite, editor of the *Edwards County Leader,* and his daughter Mattie. Not only had Dollohite not lived to cover the biggest news story in his county's history, but his newspaper shop lay in ruins, its lead type scattered like confetti by the killer storm.

Later that night the sky cleared and a full moon rose to illuminate the magnitude of the town's devastation. Leaving Laurie at her post outside of town, Owens returned to check on his family. In what remained of his house, Owens found his wife trying to staunch the flow of blood from a head wound. Nearby, her sister lay unconscious. Owens stayed with the two women until about 3 A.M., when he got word that Laurie was having trouble with the connection and needed his help. He drove back out and managed to get the line working again, but it went dead at 4:30 A.M. and stayed dead.

Several people who had been in the Ballentine Hotel had done a good job of calling for help, but relief workers had a hard time getting to Rocksprings. The torrential rains accompanying the storm had flooded the streams in the vicinity, cutting off most of the roads in the county. It took a party of doctors and Red Cross nurses from Kerrville nearly all night to get to the stricken community. Until then Rocksprings's only doctor, J. E. Rogers, "worked with the injured and dying, ministering as best he could, assisted by all residents who escaped," as one newspaper put it. Men trying to get to Rocksprings from Uvalde had to wade into Indian Creek, about 10 miles north of town, and push their cars through the water before they could proceed with the first-aid supplies they carried.

When word of the tornado reached Sonora, practically every able-bodied person in town left for Rocksprings to offer assistance, including Sam Thomas. Two days later he wrote to his mother, describing what he had witnessed:

> It was the most terrible thing I ever saw. I couldn't imagine wind could do such a thing. . . . There were dead people all stacked up in one of the banks . . . it was terrible. . . . Some of the people had big pieces of lumber through them, and they were killed most every way. . . . One little girl was carried about seven miles, but she was not dead.

Volunteers converted the Edwards County Wool and Mohair Warehouse into a hospital, along with an area behind the First State Bank. Doctors performed operations on tables covered with white oil cloth taken from nearby stores. People with lesser injuries lay on cots or blankets at the courthouse or the Ballentine Hotel.

As soon as transportation could be arranged, the more seriously wounded were taken to the nearest town with a rail connection, Camp Wood in adjoining Real County. Special trains took them from there to Uvalde and San Antonio for treatment.

The day after the tornado, the *San Angelo Standard* described the scene in Rocksprings:

The tornado took the second floor off Rocksprings High School.
COURTESY ROCKSPRINGS HOTEL

With cavalry troopers swarming through the flattened ruins of the demolished stone buildings, army airplanes flying overhead, a field hospital just off the square and a field kitchen smoking in the background, this city looked like a corner of a French battlefield of ten years ago just after a furious cannonade.

With so many people dead, survivors and relief workers had no time for elaborate funerals. Soldiers used dynamite to blast graves in the rocky ground at the cemetery, and bodies were buried as quickly as possible. The floral arrangements came from nature: The cemetery acreage abounded with colorful spring wildflowers.

Rocksprings had a population of 800 when the storm struck. Counting those killed outright and those who died later from their injuries, the tornado claimed seventy-two lives. (The same storm system killed two other people in Real County that night.) Another 205 people were treated for injuries. The Red Cross estimated property damage to be $1.2 million.

The day after the tornado, standing in the ruins of his grocery and feed store, Rocksprings mayor J. N. Lockley asked an Associated Press reporter to "convey the thanks of the citizens of Rocksprings to the whole outside world for their offers of help and their promises of aid."

Lockley had been a resident of the town since 1896, and he said that the tornado would not run him off. "Business will go on in Rocksprings," he said. "I am going to stay. . . . I believe it will be rebuilt, and rebuilt better than before."

As the mayor predicted, Rocksprings endured. Over the next five months, $750,000 went toward reconstruction. Before the town looked completely normal again, more than a million dollars had been reinvested in the community by its home and business owners.

"The determination and character which led their families to settle this isolated land gave the people of Rocksprings the strength to carry on and renew their lives and community following this nightmare of destruction," the *Texas Mohair Weekly and Rocksprings Record* declared on the fiftieth anniversary of the disaster.

THE DAY A GENERATION DIED

New London School Explosion

1937

Donald A. Sillers Jr. shifted his gaze from the hefty plaque in his hands to all the engineers seated before him in the Dallas banquet room. He stepped to the microphone, hoping that he could keep control of his voice long enough to get out what he wanted to say.

A bullet-shaped device codeveloped by his father had just been recognized by the American Society of Mechanical Engineers as a National Historic Mechanical Engineering Landmark. The proud son could have told the engineers about the company he had inherited from his father, Peerless Manufacturing, and how the roughly fireplug-size device his father had helped design had been kept in production by the company through the years despite a very slim profit margin.

Sillers also might have used the occasion to boast that the machine in question had saved countless lives over the years. Beyond that, it constituted a simple, efficient piece of engineering, having operated for a quarter of a century without needing

A monument in front of the New London School remembers explosion victims.
COURTESY NEW LONDON SCHOOL EXPLOSION MUSEUM, NLSE.ORG

any maintenance. The first of his father's machines no longer existed, but the machine receiving the landmark designation had operated from 1942 up to that very year, 1992.

Rather than say any of those things, Sillers took the audience back to a day in East Texas during the Depression, when he was a grade-school boy—the day his father suddenly ran to his car and drove off, saying that he would be back when he got back. Fighting tears, Sillers told the story.

It happened on Thursday, March 18, 1937, in New London, a fast-growing community about 120 miles east of Dallas in the booming East Texas oil field. At the town's junior-senior high school, the final bell rang each day at 3:30 P.M. A Parent-Teacher Association program had begun in the school gym at 3 P.M., and students hoped that Principal Troy Duran would follow his usual custom on PTA days and let school out thirty minutes early. But no such luck that day. Friday classes had been canceled so that students could attend a county-wide athletic competition, so the principal decided to stick to the regular Thursday schedule. That schedule changed in an instant.

At 3:15 P.M. a muffled explosion heard as far as 12 miles away literally lifted the front portion of the two-story, 30,000-square-foot school into the air. The walls of the E-shaped, yellow-brick building sucked inward almost as if the school was taking a deep breath. Then, in the words of one witness, the building began collapsing from north to south like "a row of dominoes falling." In seconds most of the walls tumbled inside the structure's foundation, with the school's red tile roof collapsing on top. A huge cloud of white dust from broken concrete mixed with red dust from the shattered tile rose above the oil derricks and pine trees. Hundreds of children and teachers lay buried under tons of concrete, steel, and bricks.

"I saw the building go up like smoke," bystander F. B. Doles later recounted. "It was just one great big puff."

Sixty yards away, eighteen-year-old Martha Harris sat in the home-economics building, one of eleven structures on the large educational campus. First she heard a "terrible roar," followed by a compression wave that shook the ground like an earthquake. Rushing to the window, she saw brick and glass showering down on the rubble that had been her school, beneath it all "my friends dying like flies."

The explosion hurled bricks as far as 500 feet. Two hundred feet from the school, a two-ton slab of concrete crushed a

1936 Chevrolet—one of fifty vehicles parked near the school that were destroyed or damaged by falling debris.

Elementary school teacher Mrs. Tom Parmley had been watching a group of children on the playground. As debris continued to rain down, she ducked into a nearby parked car, escaping injury. As soon as the deadly downpour stopped, she got out of the car and ran from child to child, trying to do what she could to stop their bleeding or otherwise comfort them. All the horrified teacher could do for one little girl was hold the child in her arms until she died.

Stunned by the enormity of what he had just witnessed, it took D. C. Saxon a few moments to recover his senses. When he did he ran to school superintendent W. C. Shaw's house and called the telephone operator in Overton, a community 4 miles southeast of the educational complex.

The superintendent, bleeding from a head wound, staggered at the edge of what had been the school, screaming "Oh my god, those poor children!" Shaw realized that some 650 to 700 children had been in the building that was now reduced to ruins. Later he would learn that his son and a niece were among the dead.

Mothers who had been on campus for the PTA meeting ran to the wreckage and frantically began trying to pull away debris, desperately hoping to get to their children. Surviving teachers and others who had been nearby soon joined the effort, many with hands bloodied by the jagged pieces of what only moments before had been a three-year-old, $300,000 educational facility.

Band director C. R. Sory had been on another part of the campus when the school building exploded. Unharmed, he loaded as many injured children into his car as he could.

Rescue workers look on as an unstable portion of the New London School collapses following the initial explosion.
COURTESY NEW LONDON SCHOOL EXPLOSION MUSEUM, NLSE.ORG

Speeding to Overton, he pulled up in front of the Western Union office and ran inside.

"The London school is blown to bits," he shouted to telegrapher A. C. Huggins. "Hundreds killed and injured! Get help."

Huggins, quickly recovering from his own shock at the news, began wiring operators in adjacent communities. Word of the explosion spread across the nation within minutes by Morse code and telephone. The nation's news services—the Associated Press, United Press, and International News—issued a "flash" on their wires, a term reserved for only the most monumental events. In Austin, Governor James V. Allred ordered all available highway patrolmen and Texas Rangers to proceed to New London.

Only an hour after the explosion, President Franklin Roosevelt wired from Warm Springs, Georgia, to inform Texas officials that he had asked the Red Cross and all federal agencies to "stand by and render every assistance in their power to the community into which the shocking tragedy has come." Across the Atlantic the tragedy touched even German dictator Adolph Hitler, who sent a telegram offering his condolences.

By 6 P.M. more than 2,000 men—many of them roughnecks from the nearby oil fields, some of them fathers of missing children—swarmed over the site, removing debris, rescuing trapped survivors, and recovering the dead and dying. One of those men was Donald Sillers, who had left his wife and son that afternoon to lend a hand. Realizing that it would be an all-night operation, volunteers and oil company personnel rigged spotlights to illuminate the scene.

At 8:30 P.M. Governor Allred declared martial law across a 5-mile area immediately around the school. National Guardsmen with fixed bayonets—augmented by Boy Scouts with unloaded rifles—enforced a perimeter around the school, allowing only medical personnel, law enforcement officers, rescue workers, relatives of missing children, and news reporters into the immediate area.

Outside the cordoned-off area, the Red Cross and Salvation Army provided sandwiches and coffee for those involved in the rescue and recovery operation. In twenty-four hours the two relief agencies served 36,000 sandwiches and enough steaming coffee to fill several tank trucks.

"It was dark and raining by the time I arrived," recalled Walter Cronkite, who as a young United Press reporter had

More than 2,000 men swarmed over the site, removing debris,
rescuing trapped survivors, and recovering the dead and dying.
COURTESY NEW LONDON SCHOOL EXPLOSION MUSEUM, NLSE.ORG

been dispatched from Dallas to New London to file stories on the tragedy. "I'll never forget the scene as I drove into the little town. I can still see those flood lights they had set up and the big oil field cranes that had been brought in to help with the removal of the rubble."

No matter how much heavy equipment rescuers brought to bear, some work had to be done by hand. Men stripped to the waist filled bushel peach baskets brick by brick, then passed the baskets from man to man to waiting dump trucks. Even reporters found themselves pressed into duty.

Seeing one small corpse after another carried from the ruins of the school proved more than one bystander could take. At 12:10 A.M. a sixty-three-year-old man dropped dead of a heart attack. Hysterical mothers fought over young bodies crushed beyond recognition, each claiming a dead child as her own.

The digging continued throughout the night. At 4 A.M. workers reached the last classroom. They found only mangled body parts of the twenty-seven students who had been in the room when the school exploded.

Working nonstop, the rescuers removed more than five million pounds of debris—and the victims beneath it—by 12:15 P.M. Friday. The bodies of 280 children and 14 adults had been found. As the mud- and blood-covered volunteers filed away from what had been the school building, National Guardsmen stepped back and snapped crisp salutes.

Most of the bodies went to a roller-skating rink in Overton operated by the American Legion. "There was row after row, and not a single child was identifiable," former Associated Press reporter Felix McKnight later recalled. "They put sheets over these kids and sprinkled formaldehyde on them. The parents would go up and down the rows, and the only way they could identify them was by the clothing."

Nearly everyone in Rusk County lost someone in the explosion or knew someone who had. "Grief was everywhere," Cronkite remembered.

In the days that followed, with their work done at the disaster site, area oil-field workers volunteered to dig graves. Area funeral homes quickly ran out of caskets, prompting a Dallas manufacturer to put his workers on around-the-clock shifts to make enough coffins to accommodate the victims. An embalming school sent its staff and students to assist in body preparation, a job often done in the open. Churches conducted up to a dozen funerals at a time, with pallbearers, preachers, and choir members moving from casket to casket. When hearses could not be had, muddy pickup trucks had to do.

Governor Allred quickly appointed a board of inquiry to determine the cause of the blast. The legislature passed a resolution requesting that the U.S. Bureau of Mines assist in the investigation.

Convening his group for the first time at 9 A.M. on March 20, the National Guard major serving as board president said, "We are not here for criminal court, but to help find the cause of the explosion and thus prevent future disasters."

After thoroughly examining the site, studying school district files, and reviewing data compiled by federal engineers, the board concluded that the explosion had been caused by natural gas leaking from pipes under the building. Undetected because it had no odor, the gas accumulated in the 64,000-cubic-foot, poorly ventilated crawl space under the floor of the building. When the oxygen-gas mixture reached just the right level of volatility, an electric spark from a sander in the basement industrial-arts shop triggered a flash fire that spread through the crawl space at 1,000 feet per second. In an instant the pressure built up to at least ninety pounds per square inch, far more than any structure could endure.

The state investigation found no fault with the school district or any of its employees. Even so, many of the parents filed suit against the oil-rich district. Some even talked of lynching the grief-stricken school superintendent, who soon resigned. A judge eventually tossed a consolidated lawsuit out of court, and the anger that so often follows grief slowly settled into acceptance.

*Parents, family members, and local residents gather for a memorial
service at what was left of the school.*
COURTESY NEW LONDON SCHOOL EXPLOSION MUSEUM, NLSE.ORG

Two years later the people of Rusk and the surrounding
counties gathered for the dedication of a 32-foot-tall pink gran-
ite monument at the school site. Children throughout the
United States donated their nickels and dimes to pay for the
$21,300 cenotaph, which still stands. Two columns support a
twenty-ton block that features life-size representations of ten
children and two teachers. Carved in the enduring igneous
rock are 294 names, those of most of the students and teachers who died in the tragedy. But the actual number of fatalities
ran higher.

Like all schools, the New London school kept daily atten-
dance records, but they were lost or destroyed in the explosion.
The only surviving list of students had been made on the first
day of classes the previous September and filed at the Rusk
County courthouse in the county school superintendent's
office. Since the area was in the midst of an oil boom, new students were arriving all the time.

Later research by Mollie Ward, an explosion survivor and
director of the New London School Museum, located 319 death
certificates for children and adults killed outright or mortally
injured in the explosion. Regardless of what figure is used, the
New London explosion remains the worst school disaster in
U.S. history.

The New London explosion killed a generation, but it also
brought about several changes intended to prevent something
like that from ever happening again. Later in the spring of
1937, the Texas Legislature passed the Texas Engineering Registration Act. The law mandated that engineers register with
the state, a process requiring proof of professional credentials.
The legislature also created the Texas Board of Architectural
Examiners to oversee the examination, registration, education,
and professional regulation of architects, landscape architects,
and interior designers. But the most important measure taken
came later that summer when the Texas Railroad Commission
approved an order requiring that natural gas intended for
domestic or industrial use be odorized.

That's where Sillers's father got involved a second time.
Images of dead children forever seared into his memory, he
worked with Alexander Clarke to develop a device they called
a metering gas odorizer. It injected a precise amount of a
pungent chemical into natural gas flowing through it into

transmission lines. Sillers and Clarke filed for a patent on the device on June 18, 1939.

Their invention did not reduce the explosive qualities of natural gas, but it offered industrialized society something that the children of New London never had: warning of a gas leak. With tears in his eyes, Sillers's son concluded his acceptance speech by telling the engineers what his father had done when he finally got home after working all night and half the next day at the scene of the disaster: He gathered his son in his arms for a long, silent hug.

DEADLIEST FIRE IN TEXAS

Houston's Gulf Hotel Blaze

1943

No one knew how soon World War II would end, but by 1943 Germany and Japan clearly faced defeat. The third Axis power, Italy, had surrendered and Allied military leaders secretly worked on plans for the invasion of Nazi-controlled France.

Hundreds of thousands of Texans served in the Army, Navy, and Marines in the European and Pacific theaters, but the fuel and equipment needed to support the American war machine came from the home front. Few areas in the nation played a more critical role than Southeast Texas.

Houston, which with more than 400,000 residents was already Texas's largest city, grew larger by the day. The boom had begun in 1940, when·the U.S. War Department awarded the Humble Oil and Refining Company a $12 million contract to produce toluene, an ingredient for high explosives. Shell Oil Company also began production of the chemical, adding new infrastructure and employees.

General Tire and Rubber Company soon had a large plant
operating in Baytown. Massive storage tanks, towering chemical distilleries, and mazes of pipe lined the 50-mile ship channel connecting the Port of Houston to the Gulf of Mexico as
new chemical plants and refineries went up or existing facilities expanded their plants to meet wartime needs. Factories
that had catered to oil-field needs converted their operations to
produce everything from mortar-shell fins to machine-gun
tripods.

The Houston Shipbuilding Corporation landed a Liberty
Ship contract, eventually building a complete 7,500-ton
freighter every fifty-three days. The shipyard operated around
the clock, employing more than 20,000 men. Chambers of
commerce soon began referring to the Southeast Texas area
bounded by Houston, Beaumont–Port Arthur, and Freeport as
the "Golden Triangle."

From all across the nation, men came to the area looking
for the steady jobs that they had not been able to find since the
Depression. One of them was fifty-three-year-old Walter L.
Campbell. Too old for the military and not inclined toward
blue-collar work, he got hired as a night clerk at the Gulf Hotel
in downtown Houston. He pulled a twelve-hour shift, working
the front desk from 4 P.M. until 4 A.M. Coffee, cigarettes, and
the promise of regular pay got him through each night.

Houston had 106 tourist courts and hotels. Several of them,
most notably the grand Rice Hotel, enjoyed the reputation of
being the finest in the South. But the Gulf Hotel was far from
fine. Occupying the top two floors of an old three-story building at Louisiana and Preston Streets, the hotel had eighty-
seven beds that rented for 40 cents a night, plus fifty cots
available at half that cost. Despite the somewhat seedy accom-

modations, the hotel enjoyed a brisk business. On the night of September 6, Campbell's guest registry listed 133 names.

Around 12:15 A.M. on Tuesday, September 7, eight hours into his shift, Campbell heard someone yelling that he smelled smoke. The clerk left the desk and started checking the rooms on the second floor.

When Campbell opened the door to room 201, smoke poured out. It looked like the renter, C. G. Smith, had fallen asleep with a cigarette in his hand. Seeing a smoldering area about the size of his hand on the bed, the clerk doused the fire with a bucket of water. He then pulled the burned sheet off the bed and put it with the dirty linens in a storage closet across the hall. Whether the groggy guest whose carelessness had led to the incident got another sheet was not reported. (Another account says that Campbell and several others dragged the mattress across the hall to the closet.) Thinking that he had handled the situation, Campbell returned to the front desk, and Smith went back to sleep.

Around 12:45 A.M., as Campbell sat working on the books, he again heard someone yelling from a room. This time the commotion came from the third floor.

Climbing the narrow steps, Campbell met a man griping that someone had been shining a flashlight, disturbing a room packed with men on cots. Campbell walked around looking for the wiseacre with the flashlight, but no one seemed to know who it was.

Just as he reached the foot of the stairs on his return to the second floor, the clerk saw flames shooting from the wall behind the front desk. This time, Campbell knew, a container of water would not be enough to put out the fire. Running to a pay phone in the hall, he called the fire department. It was 12:50 A.M.

Six blocks away the first engine company pulled out of the Central Fire Station with its sirens screaming. Deputy Chief Grover Cleveland Adams could see the reflected light from the fire as he left the station.

"After I made the call," Campbell later reported, "I started rousing people on the second floor. Then I called the people on the third floor and told them the hotel was on fire." The clerk could hear men shouting and running upstairs.

"I stayed there on the second floor . . . until things started falling all around me," Campbell later told police. "I helped several old men get downstairs."

Indeed, many of the renters were elderly, trying to get by on meager relief checks. But a fair number of younger defense plant workers also lived at the hotel, unable to find an apartment or a room at one of the better hotels. One of those men was twenty-year-old Irvin Duesterhoff. He had gone to a movie that night after getting off work. Back from the theater only a short time, he had been lying in bed reading when he smelled smoke.

Rushing to dress, he grabbed someone else's pants. "I yelled to some of the men next to my room and then found my way to a fire escape," he told a reporter later that morning.

On the way to the fire exit, Duesterhoff saw an older man sitting on the side of his bed, flames engulfing him. "I couldn't get to him, and he just sat there rocking back and forth as he burned to death," the shaken young man said. Unable to do more, he continued to the exit.

Meanwhile, Campbell encountered a solid wall of fire on the second floor when he returned to try to get more men out. Running downstairs to save his own life, the clerk met the first fire trucks and policemen to reach the scene.

Police homicide captain C. A. Martindale happened to be only three blocks from the hotel when the blaze broke out. When the captain pulled his car to the curb at the burning building, he saw a man making his way down the fire escape.

"His clothing was on fire," the officer told the *Houston Press* a few hours later. "He got to within five or six feet of the pavement and then jumped. He landed on his bare feet and kept running. I tried to catch him [to smother the flames] but he disappeared."

Martindale watched as the fire raced through the old building. A veteran officer, he knew that it would be full of transients ranging from the honest but poor to skid-row bums lucky enough to have come up with enough change for a night off the street.

Ted Fields, director of the Harris County Emergency Corps, arrived shortly after Captain Martindale. He saw the fire escape on the Preston Street side of the hotel jammed with guests. Some of them had only one leg and were trying to get down the iron walkway with crutches.

Firefighters unlimbered their hoses and pumped multiple streams of high-pressure water on the burning structure, but they knew that they could not get inside to try to rescue any of the occupants. Sirens wailed in the darkness as the fire department rolled more equipment on a general alarm.

Choking and blinded by smoke, one man trapped inside the hotel opted to jump from the windows rather than burn to death. Fields ran to check on that man, only to be hit in the shoulder by another body that hurtled down, knocking Fields to the sidewalk. One man made it half way out a window when the window sash came crashing down on his body, trapping him. As firemen watched helplessly, the man burned to death, screaming in agony until the merciful onset of unconsciousness.

Duesterhoff had made it halfway down the fire escape when a man fell past him, barely missing him. "He had jumped from the third floor," Duesterhoff told a reporter. "The man was moaning as his body fell. I looked down as he bounced on the sidewalk. . . . Some sailors grabbed him and carried him to an ambulance. I don't know whether or not he was killed."

Firemen finally got the blaze under control around 3 A.M. Then they began removing bodies. Many of the victims lay in a pile on the second floor, near a window leading to the fire escape. They found thirty-eight victims inside the hotel; two had died outside from jumping, and fifteen died in hospitals.

Later that morning, Houston police began to identify the dead. The easiest way to do that, they realized, was to first learn the names of the survivors. Since they also had to find out how the fire started, all available detectives started taking statements from many of the seventy-eight roomers who had managed to escape.

"I woke up choking and turned the light on," seventy-year-old D. J. Brown told a detective. "The smoke was so thick I had to feel my way to the door. I heard men running in the hall. Some of them were crying for help in their rooms."

Brown said that he shouted a warning to a couple of his friends in adjoining rooms before managing to make it downstairs. "I don't know whether they got out or not," he continued in his statement. "I [walked] around for hours trying to find them. I guess they're up there burned to death."

Campbell and Duesterhoff had done all they could to get people out of the blazing building, but both agreed that the real hero was Ben Taylor, another hotel resident.

Houston firefighters train their hoses on the burning hotel, their faces retouched by a staff artist later that day in one of the city's afternoon newspapers.

HOUSTON METROPOLITAN RESEARCH CENTER, COURTESY HOUSTON PUBLIC LIBRARY, HOUSTON

"Taylor risked his life to help others to the stairway and the fire escapes," Duesterhoff told the *Houston Press*. "He kept running back to get some of the older men. Several times he had to stop and beat the flames from his clothes. The last time I saw him he was tearing off his blazing shirt. I guess he saved the lives of twenty men."

The determined rescuer suffered only minor burns.

As detectives continued to interview survivors, one man asked if he could use the officer's telephone. Like many of those who had gotten out of the hotel, the man wore only a sheet. As the detective looked on, he shouted into the phone: "Listen, boss, if you want me to show up for work this morning you'd better send me some clothes. I'm naked as Gandhi." Within an hour the man had a set of work clothes, and soon he was back on the job.

Though most of the charred bodies had been removed from the gutted hotel by the end of the day Tuesday, investigators found a body in a washroom on Wednesday and another— the final victim to be located—at 10:30 A.M. Thursday, thirty hours after the fire.

Shortly after the beginning of the war, Houston city officials had worked with the military to develop contingency plans in the event of mass deaths from air raids. Such raids never materialized, but city workers began making arrangements to carry out one grim aspect of the war plan: a mass burial.

Twenty-three of the fifty-five fire victims had not been identified; thirteen others, though their names had been determined, had been indigent. City officials decided that these thirty-six victims would be buried together. On Thursday morning a large trench-digging machine cut into the ground at South Park Cemetery, opening a grave 100 feet long and 8 feet wide.

The victims had not been from the top tier of Houston society, but many had served their nation during World War I or put in long hours at area defense plants. "Others," the *Houston Press* reported, "were just tired old men who had no place to go, no relatives, no interest in life except a cot and a long day of chatter with their buddies." Civic leaders believed that the unidentified men who died in the hotel fire deserved more than paupers' funerals, regardless of what their stations in life had been.

The American Red Cross's national disaster relief committee said that it would pay for each of the thirty-six burials. When word of that got out, local funeral directors, local florists, and the cemetery manager agreed to reduce their charges by 50 percent, giving each victim a silk-lined casket and a funeral service that normally would cost $240.

On the afternoon of September 9, a procession of thirty-six hearses (escorted by Houston motorcycle police officers) traveled Alvin Road to the cemetery. American Legionnaires and members of the Texas Defense Guard served as pallbearers, carrying each of the flower-draped coffins to the mass grave, an opening lined on one side by small U.S. and American Legion flags.

"War heroes could have had no more elaborate funeral," one *Houston Press* reporter observed in his coverage of the burial.

Mayor Otis Massey, the city manager, council members, Red Cross nurses, fire survivors, and several hundred Houstonians who had come to pay their respects stood by as Catholic, Protestant, and Jewish clergy conducted services.

"A great problem confronts us here," Reverend P. A. Fee said, "the problem of the betterment of our city. It is our duty that we show our love for our fellow men, especially those less fortunate than us, by correcting the cause of this terrible catastrophe."

By the end of the week, investigators concluded that the fire had started in the linen closet behind the front desk. That's where the night clerk had taken the sheet he had removed from the bed in room 201, just across the hall. Though Campbell told investigators that he had doused the flaming sheet, it apparently rekindled after he tossed it into the linen closet.

The man whose cigarette ignited the sheet died in the fire. A Harris County grand jury looked into the circumstances leading to the blaze but returned no indictments. However, Houston city officials and council members struggled with the safety issue for several months after the disaster. As Councilman M. C. Gaines explained, bringing all of the city's hotels and apartments into compliance with even the existing fire code was not as simple as it seemed, especially in light of the wartime housing shortage.

"Something ought to be done," he said, "but if we just closed these places up, those folks [defense workers and those with little income] wouldn't have any place to live. I think some [code] changes should be made. We must do everything in our power to prevent another Gulf Hotel tragedy."

The city fire marshal's office had been studying low-cost lodging even before the fire. Fire-prevention inspectors checked seventy rooming houses and "second or third rate" hotels from August 23 to September 12, 1943, finding 350 hazards. Defective electrical wiring or appliances topped the list, followed by accumulations of flammable materials. In August alone, inspectors found forty-five faulty fire escapes and forty-eight improperly hung exit doors.

Three days after the fire, a city council committee headed by Councilman Spencer Robinson conducted its own inspection, visiting six low-rent downtown hotels that charged as little as 15 cents a night for an iron cot in a crowded room with only one washbasin and no toilet for sixty men.

"I knew that conditions were bad at some of these places but I never dreamed that we would find some of these things," Councilman John Bell told a reporter.

At one hotel the councilmen discovered that the fire escape could be reached only through a room that one woman rented by the week. "I always put a chair against the door at night," she told the city men. Checking another hotel, inspectors found that the "fire escape" consisted of ropes hung near the second-floor windows. In another hotel the fire exit had been blocked by a bed.

Accompanied by the fire marshal, the elected officials found false floors that had been built without a city permit and narrow stairs that only one person at a time could use. Stacked furniture also blocked hallways. Overall, the councilmen concluded, conditions were "deplorable."

With three hospitalized survivors remaining in critical condition, the fire marshal said that he would file charges against fifteen hotel operators if they did not immediately correct the fire hazards identified by his inspectors. In a similar inspection blitz, health inspectors visited a dozen locations. They noted overcrowded conditions and inadequate sanitary facilities at all but one of those lodging places.

Rooting out violations of existing fire safety and health standards helped, but the city's fire code also needed work. As the fire marshal told the council's investigative committee, the code did not require fire escapes for hotels with only two floors.

Eventually the city council voted to bring Houston's building and fire codes up to more rigorous safety standards, and the fire marshal's office continued its increased enforcement efforts. In addition, the health department's crackdown on unsanitary conditions in low-cost lodging places continued.

Though the story stayed on the front page of Houston's dailies for weeks, the Gulf Hotel fire is one of Texas's least known disasters. In the more than six decades since the tragedy, nothing even close in terms of loss of life has occurred at a Houston hotel.

FUEL TO THE FIRE

Texas City Explosion
1947

Julio Luna knew his way around a Liberty ship. He had served on the USS *Starr King* during World War II, until a Japanese submarine torpedoed the freighter out from under him, and he later served as a gunner's mate on the USS *Hornet.*

After the war Luna returned to his family in the Mexican-American barrio of abandoned boxcars near Texas City and found work as a longshoreman.

On the unseasonably cool morning of Wednesday, April 16, 1947, Luna stood around with the other dockworkers waiting for the early morning fog to lift. He had worked for two straight days loading one-hundred-pound bags of ammonium nitrate—commercial fertilizer—into the holds of the *Grandcamp,* and with another 1,200 bags yet to be loaded, he expected a nice little pay packet to take home.

The *Grandcamp* had started life as the Liberty ship USS *Benjamin R. Curtis* and served in the Pacific theater during World War II. Liberty ships were a class of hastily built, simply designed cargo vessels. Their designation originated with the USS *Patrick Henry,* named for the patriot who said "Give me

liberty or give me death." President Franklin Roosevelt dubbed
Liberty ships "ugly ducklings," but they got the job done. War
production plants churned out more than 2,700 before the war's
end in 1945, with some 200 lost in action. After the war the government declared the remaining Liberty ships surplus and
offered them for sale domestically and to former Allies overseas.

Flying French colors, the *Grandcamp* had docked at Texas
City in the fog on Sunday night, April 13. It was the last stop
before she sailed for her homeport of Brest. The holds already
carried more than 9,000 bags of shelled peanuts; sixteen cases
of small arms ammunition; bales of sisal twine and cotton; and
heavy oil-well, refrigeration, and farm machinery.

With a population of 18,000, Texas City had been a major
defense-industry town during World War II and did not miss a
beat after V-J Day. Discharged servicemen came home, wives
left the airplane and ship factories, the baby boom began, and
many ex-GIs went to work in one of the numerous petrochemical plants along the Texas coast.

Now the United States found itself in a different kind of
war—a "cold war," as British Prime Minister Winston
Churchill called it—with the Soviet Union and Communism.
Part of President Harry Truman's strategy to prevent further
expansion of Communism was to help the war-ravaged people
in Western Europe rebuild their shattered economies as
quickly as possible. The fertilizer being loaded into the *Grandcamp* constituted part of that effort.

Luna lowered himself into Hold 4 and started shifting
heavy six-ply paper bags from wooden pallets. Over the rank
odor of chemical fertilizer, Luna caught a whiff of something
that smelled like it was burning. He sniffed the air nervously
and then yelled, "Fire in the hold!"

Prior to the explosion huge plumes of colored smoke billowed from the burning Grandcamp.   COURTESY CENTER FOR AMERICAN HISTORY, UNIVERSITY OF TEXAS, AUSTIN

Assuming that the fire could be quickly doused, Luna's dock boss lowered two one-gallon jars of drinking water. Quickly Luna sloshed both jars alongside the bags, but it proved a waste of time. Luna guessed that the fire was smoldering several bags deep, as wisps of acrid smoke quickly rose next to another pallet.

Now flames could be seen. Two of the French crew aimed soda acid sprays at the pallets. The flames died down for a moment but quickly licked up the side of Hold 4's starboard bulkhead. Luna had seen enough. He scrambled out of the hold, onto Pier O, and walked away. Good money was not worth dying for.

Curtis Trahan, like most of the men in Texas City, had served in the military during the war. He had survived the Battle of the Bulge, though badly wounded, and had spent months in a hospital before coming home to his wife, Edna, and his two young sons. Trahan returned to Texas determined to do what he could to make his hometown better for everyone. He knew that he had no hope of changing segregation, but he might be able to lessen the hardships in the Mexican-American barrio and the black neighborhood called Shanty-town or "the Bottoms."

Trahan had served as mayor of Texas City for almost a year. Most people agreed that he had good ideas, but they all cost money—something the town did not have. Texas City Terminal Railway, Monsanto Chemical, Humble Oil, Atlantic Pipeline Company, and the other giant industries all operated outside the city limits and did not pay taxes. Without a strong tax base, Trahan held little hope for Texas City's future.

That morning Mayor Trahan took his younger son and his neighbors' two daughters to school and then headed straight for the docks. He had heard that there was a fire in the hold of one of the ships but that it seemed to be under control. From the docks Trahan drove 3 blocks to the city barn to check on road equipment and trucks.

Moments before, Henry J. "Mike" Mikeska had parked near the dock and looked things over before heading to his nearby office. A civil engineering graduate of Texas A&M University, Mikeska had been with Texas City Railway Terminal Company for thirty years and had worked his way up to president.

The Company, as it was called, "made" Texas City. Back in 1891, while the Myers brothers from Minnesota hunted duck in the coastal marshlands, they looked around and decided that the area would make a good deepwater port. The brothers bought up the swampy land and gave the place a name as big as all of Texas.

The Texas City port remained open even after the devastating Galveston hurricane of 1900. The federal government set up a customs house, and Texas City docks increased in number to handle oil from the Spindletop discovery. The Texas City Refining Company was chartered in 1908, and Texas crude became the terminal's major export. By 1921 the company controlled everything coming into or leaving the port.

Outside his office Mikeska stood and talked for a few minutes with Pete Suderman, the longshoremen's union representative. Mikeska wanted good men working the docks. Six to eight hundred tons of ammonium nitrate remained to be loaded on the *Grandcamp;* the rain had caused delays, and delays cost the company money.

Mikeska walked briskly to his office, eager to get to work. He liked his job, and it kept him busy. Texas City ranked as the fourth-largest port on the Gulf of Mexico and tenth or eleventh in the United States, depending on who was counting. The port handled some 25,000 ships a year, and Mikeska viewed the vessels as his personal responsibility. Just as he sat down at his desk, he heard a ship's alarm whistle.

"There's a fire down at the French ship," someone said.

Looking from his office window, Mikeska could see three cargo vessels: the *Grandcamp,* the *High Flyer,* and the *Wilson B. Keene.* Plumes of peach-colored smoke poured from one of the ships. Realizing the danger of having a burning ship at dockside, Mikeska wanted it pulled out to open waters as quickly as possible.

The workers of Southwestern Bell Telephone Company had been on strike since April 7, but Mikeska got an operator, phoned Galveston, and ordered two tugboats to haul the burning ship away from the pier. Then he left his office and quickly walked the few hundred yards from his office to Pier O.

The *Grandcamp* had taken on most of her cargo at the Port of Houston, but the commercial fertilizer had to be loaded at Texas City. Port officials in Houston prohibited the loading of ammonium nitrate on their docks because studies showed the substance to be "unstable."

When Luna had shouted "Fire!" *Grandcamp* captain Charles de Guillebon came on deck and talked to his officers and engineers. They had lost enough time in port as it was, waiting for the drizzle to let up so they could load the remaining fertilizer.

Afraid that water from fire hoses would damage the *Grandcamp*'s cargo, the captain instructed his men to batten down the hatches and turn on the ship's steam system to smother any flames in Hold 4. Just as an added precaution, the captain ordered stevedores to begin removing the cases of small arms ammunition from Hold 5.

At 8:20 A.M. Captain de Guillebon ordered the ship's whistle to sound the alarm—three short blasts and one long one. A minute or two later, the Monsanto Company's siren echoed the alarm. The longshoremen and the French sailors began to drift on down the dock, walking away from the smoking ship.

The town's curiosity seekers took their places; fire on the docks always drew a crowd. A hundred or more people, including some schoolchildren cutting classes, gathered to watch the beautiful plumes of colored smoke as they rose ever higher. The *Grandcamp* began to heave and groan from the increasing heat.

At the sound of the alarms, Henry Baumgartner, chief of the Texas City Volunteer Fire Department, stepped out of his office in the Texas City Terminal Railway. He saw the smoke coming

An L. L. Cook Co. postcard showing wreckage along the waterfront following the April 16, 1947 Texas City explosion. FROM THE AUTHOR'S COLLECTION

from Pier O, and with twenty years of experience warning him that this was no ordinary fire, he shouted for a general alarm.

Within minutes two of the town's fire trucks rolled up alongside the burning ship, followed by the other two, and twenty-seven of the volunteers reported. Baumgartner told the men to pump water from the harbor to fight the fire. Inside the vessel an inferno raged. The *Grandcamp*'s decks were so hot from the fire below that the oily water streaming from the fire hoses vaporized on contact. Even so, at 9:12 A.M., the fire chief and his men climbed aboard the vessel to fight the fire more aggressively.

At that moment an officer aboard the *William B. Keene* stepped on deck to take some photographs of the *Grandcamp*. About the time the officer tripped the shutter of his camera, the *Grandcamp* exploded, sending hot metal and debris into the air amid a multicolored mushroom-shaped cloud that rose 2,000 feet. The ship's one-and-a-half-ton anchor sailed 2 miles through the air. The shock wave from the explosion tossed the *High Flyer* into the *Wilson B. Keene* like a toy boat.

The blast, which many initially believed had been an atomic bomb dropped by the Russians, killed or badly injured anyone within 1,000 to 1,500 feet of Pier O. Mike Mikeska disappeared, his body never to be found. Warehouse O became a pile of rubble. The explosion wrecked the nearby Monsanto plant, killing more than 150 employees out of 450 on that shift and injuring many more. Hundreds of others—including many of the spectators—suffered burns, cuts from shards of broken glass, or ruptured eardrums from the force of the blast.

Hearing and feeling the explosion, a Southwestern Bell supervisor plugged into the toll circuit to Houston and pleaded: "For God's sake, send the Red Cross! There's been a big explosion and thousands are injured!"

The waterfront sustained the greatest damage, but downtown Texas City did not escape. Windows blew out, roofs and walls collapsed, and electrical power and water lines were disrupted along Sixth Street, Texas Avenue, and the cross streets.

If anything saved Texas City from an even greater death toll, it was the number of veterans, trained nurses, and first-aid volunteers who had served during the war. Even in shock, they rallied to get the injured to one of Texas City's three clinics. When those quickly overflowed, the wounded were taken to the city auditorium.

Medical personnel from Galveston and Houston rushed to Texas City. The Texas Department of Public Safety and law enforcement agencies from surrounding counties sent every man who could be spared to augment Texas City's seventeen-member police department. Volunteer undertakers and embalmers began to deal with the many mangled dead.

Around 5:30 P.M. Fourth Army General Jonathan Wainwright arrived from Fort Sam Houston with emergency medical supplies and a field kitchen. Camp Wallace, a deactivated army facility near Texas City, provided a temporary refuge for the homeless.

The Texas City disaster made the biggest news since the end of World War II. Newspaper reporters and radio announcers poured into town. Staffers from the *Texas City Sun* rushed to nearby Goose Creek (now Baytown) and published an extra on the presses of the *Goose Creek Sun*. In the coming days, with power restored, the *Texas City Sun* would publish lists of the dead, injured, and missing as well as pleas from families who had become separated.

In the chaos resulting from the explosion of the *Grandcamp*, the *High Flyer* had been all but forgotten. The force of the *Grandcamp*'s explosion blew off the *High Flyer*'s cargo hatches and tore the vessel from its moorings, allowing it to drift against the *Wilson B. Keene*. Hopelessly entangled by debris from what had been the *Grandcamp*, neither ship could move.

The four tugs ordered from Galveston did not reach Texas City until almost 9:30 P.M. By then, fire sounding like a volcano rumbled deep within the *High Flyer*. Chains attached to the *High Flyer* failed to budge the ship. Workmen boarded it and used an acetylene torch in an attempt to free the anchor chain, but nothing worked.

Finally the workers decided that they could do nothing more. Crews reboarded their tugs a little after 1 A.M. April 17 and began to cast off for Galveston, and that's when the *High Flyer* exploded. The *Wilson B. Keene* broke in half and sank.

Many initially believed the blast had been an atomic bomb dropped by the Russians. This L. L. Cook Co. postcard illustrates why.
FROM THE AUTHOR'S COLLECTION

Witnesses later said that the blast from the *High Flyer* sounded far worse than that of the *Grandcamp*. The night air may have magnified the sound over the water, or the burning sulfur in Holds 2 and 4 may have contaminated the 961 tons of ammonium nitrate in Hold 3. Although casualties from the *High Flyer* explosion were light, the blast sent more automobiles, railroad cars, and oil storage tanks into the air and frightened already shell-shocked townspeople.

The grim work of recovering and identifying bodies continued. Meanwhile, relief efforts around the world led to much-needed donations. Schoolchildren mailed pennies to "The Children of Texas City." A well-known club owner from Galveston organized a fund-raising tour of his most popular entertainers: radio and movie stars Frank Sinatra, Alice Faye, Phil Silvers, and Red Skelton.

Monsanto Chemical quickly announced that it would rebuild. The plant was a large part of Texas City's economy, and the word brought some comfort to the survivors.

Not until weeks later did relief workers find the last body. The official estimate stood at 581 dead, but there may have been more. Many bodies were unidentifiable or—like Mike Mikeska—simply never found. Since many residents of the barrio and the Bottoms had no utility service and lived in rent houses, no accurate death count could be made in those areas.

On Sunday morning, June 22, Texas City finally gathered to bury sixty-three unknown dead—blacks, whites, or Hispanics, no one knew—in a single mass grave. Seven different clergymen participated in the funeral service. In a town that had been as segregated as any in Texas, some healing had finally begun.

"THEY'RE CATCHING HELL"

Waco Tornado

1953

George Huebner flipped the power switch and waited for the tubes in the piano-size radar set to warm up. With reports of stormy weather farther west in the state, this seemed like a good afternoon to spend some time on his graduate research project, an investigation into the use of radar to observe weather.

Earlier that day, May 11, 1953, the U.S. Weather Bureau in New Orleans had warned of severe thunderstorms and possible tornadoes inside a large trapezoid of Texas defined by the cities of Wichita Falls, Big Spring, San Angelo, and Waco. At 2:30 P.M. a tornado had cut across the northern portion of the West Texas city of San Angelo, killing 11 people and injuring 159.

Now, as Huebner sat in the electrical engineering building at Texas A&M University in College Station looking at the screen of the converted World War II apparatus, he could tell that heavy weather had developed over Central Texas. On the screen's 80-mile marker, he could see a big blob of white. That, he knew, represented radio waves bouncing off the heavy rain associated with a powerful thunderstorm.

"Man, they're catching hell up there in Waco," Huebner thought.

At 4:32 P.M. he tripped the shutter on a camera attached to the radar, a set similar to one that he had used for different purposes during the war. The screen now displayed five large echoes over Waco, a city of 85,000 halfway between Dallas and Austin. Huebner did not realize it, but he had just photographed a killer tornado.

South of Waco at Lorena, volunteer weather observer T. H. McBrayer did not need radar to understand that a severe storm approached. At 3:55 P.M., a little more than a half hour earlier, he had stood on a hill watching the boiling cumulonimbus clouds develop into a giant thunderstorm. Twenty minutes later, a law enforcement officer south of Waco saw a huge tornado drop from the threatening skies, but before he could get a call through to the McLennan County Sheriff's office, the telephone line went dead. The giant funnel demolished a farmhouse and then moved on. Roaring north, it destroyed a few farm buildings outside tiny Hewitt, about 8 miles from Waco. Two hours before sunset, the sky had turned nearly as dark as night as the storm bore down on the city.

Scattering cars at the Waco traffic circle on the southern edge of the city, the funnel continued to grow in size and strength. It moved into the Bell's Hill neighborhood, dropping baseball-size hail and turning houses into piles of lumber and sheetrock. Churning through the Cotton Palace Park, the tornado—more than 2 blocks wide—took dead aim on the heart of the city.

With an increased speed of 30 mph, the twister had begun to kill. Two teenage boys lay dead, crushed when a concrete wall toppled onto the underground locker room at Cotton

Palace Park, where they had taken shelter. Closer to downtown, the ferocious wind dislodged a rooftop water tank at a warehouse near Fifth and Jackson Streets; the tank broke through five floors of concrete and killed a custodian in the basement. On Eighth Street the tornado peeled the brick wall from a warehouse, burying a man and his wife who happened to be driving by in their convertible.

Moments before, Ted Lucenay had left the downtown doctor's office where he worked to walk across the street and buy a copy of that afternoon's newspaper. Glancing at the front page on his way back, he saw a story that West Texas had experienced some violent spring weather, but someone with the Waco office of the Weather Bureau said that "there was no cause for alarm in Central Texas." Should any tornadoes develop, forecaster C. A. Anderson said, "They would be west of Waco if they did strike." Indeed, in its printed material, the chamber of commerce bragged about an old Indian legend that Waco enjoyed eternal immunity from tornadoes.

Lucenay did not get a chance to finish reading the story or ponder local folklore. Shortly after he walked back to his office building, it collapsed. Buried under bricks and other debris, Lucenay could barely breathe. He began to think that he might never see his three kids and pregnant wife again.

On the other side of the wall he could hear his coworker, a nurse. She had been hit by a desk. "I could not see her," Lucenay recalled. "We talked through the wall, but I heard her until she took her dying breath."

On the courthouse square, customers and barbers in the Jockey Club barbershop took shelter under a stairway as the windows popped out and the mirrors inside shattered. "Lord, have mercy," barber Benny Frank Smith prayed.

At Fifth Street and Austin Avenue, the city's center, shoppers taking advantage of a sale on baby furniture crowded the five-story R. T. Dennis Furniture Company. While customers looked for bargains, on the second floor longtime employee Lillie Matkins answered the firm's switchboard with a familiar, cheerful voice. At 4:37 P.M., busily connecting to the extensions of various store executives to set up a meeting, the telephone operator wondered why the store's lights kept flickering on and off. Just as it occurred to her that it must have something to do with the weather, she heard an unworldly roar. The lights died again, and this time they did not come back on. In the darkness Matkins realized that she was falling. The building had collapsed on itself.

When the furniture store caved in, bricks rained down on the Torrance Recreation Hall across the alley. Local high school football player Don Hansard had just sunk an 11 ball when the lights failed. Then the ceiling came down, killing eighteen people and trapping twenty-seven others. Hansard survived, but a friend there with him did not.

Next door at Fifth Street and Franklin Avenue, the four-story Padgitt Building, another of the city's older downtown buildings, also lay in ruins. In the square block bordered by Fourth and Fifth Streets and Austin and Franklin Avenues, searchers eventually would recover fifty-six bodies, the highest concentration of fatalities in the city.

Still, it could have been worse. Inside the nearby Joy Theater, one hundred people had been watching Robert Mitchum in *The Lusty Men*. When the tornado hit, the screen went black with the sudden loss of electricity. Seconds later the high, arched ceiling crashed down. Luckily for the audience, the ceiling's arches provided just enough structural support to stop it a few feet above their heads.

People in the twenty-two-story American Life Tower had fate on their side as well. For years the tower had been the tallest building west of the Mississippi. That distinction had been eclipsed by 1953, but the skyscraper remained Waco's highest structure.

At the first sign of rain, workers in the high-rise had shut their windows despite the stifling heat and humidity. They would have had a perfect vantage point to see the tornado, but the heavy rain hid it from view even as it spun straight toward their building. Fortunately for the scores of people inside, the building's architect had designed the structure to be flexible in extreme winds. The skyscraper suddenly oscillated like a straight-edge ruler twanged by a child, but when the tornado moved past, it still stood.

The tornado continued across the Brazos River, destroying homes in East Waco and blowing away a major portion of an elementary school. Fortunately, the children had already gone home for the day.

Less than fifteen minutes after hitting downtown Waco, the tornado dissipated over the small community of Axtell, just north of the ravaged city.

East of downtown, at Baylor University, Dr. Robert G. Packhard's physics class listened to a guest speaker talking about the use of weather balloons to predict storms. Then the lights went out. When the power did not come back on, Packhard dismissed the class and drove downtown to see what had happened.

"Waco looked like a city that had been bombed," he recalled. "Debris was everywhere."

The disastrous Waco tornado of 1953 was the impetus for the nation's first weather radar network.   FROM THE AUTHOR'S COLLECTION

Tommy Turner, Waco correspondent for the *Dallas Morning News,* had been downtown only ten minutes before the tornado hit.

"You couldn't get within about four blocks of the middle of town," he recalled. "The entire R.T. Dennis Co. Building had . . . slid into the street, and the bricks next to the curb were between five to twenty feet deep."

Turner saw cars—and the dead people inside them—flattened to only 2 feet above the pavement. Water ran down Austin Avenue 6 inches deep, with dangling electric lines shooting sparks overhead. The rotten smell of escaping natural gas filled the air. The scene, Turner said, "almost overwhelmed me."

Many had died inside the Dennis furniture store building, but middle-aged Lillie Matkins somehow had survived. For nearly an hour she lay in darkness, pinned beneath tons of debris, barely able to breathe.

"I kept screaming, 'help, help,'" she recalled, "but I couldn't get any response. I asked the Lord if I couldn't get out to take me then. I was ready."

Finally, about an hour after the furniture store's collapse, Matkins heard male voices somewhere above her and began shouting as loudly as she could. This time, someone heard her and yelled back to ask if she was hurt. No, she replied, but she could not move any part of her body except her feet.

At 9:30 P.M., five hours after the tornado, rescuers continued to remove rubble in their effort to get to Matkins. Another hour and forty-five minutes passed, and Matkins struggled to breathe. "I want air," she called out in a weaker voice. Firemen brought an oxygen tank into the wreckage and passed an oxygen mask to her through a narrow hole.

At 2:30 A.M. rescuers began using a gasoline-powered saw to cut some of the timbers blocking their access to the woman. Worried that the whirling blade might cut her instead, Matkins yelled, "I've been here ten hours—a little longer won't hurt."

Nearly three hours later, a rescue worker who had crawled into the debris to remove obstructions had to come out, weak from lack of oxygen. Someone else took his place, and by 6:30 A.M. a long rope dropped into a cleared pit adjacent to Matkins's location. "If you will only let me tell you what to do," she pleaded, but the rescuers already knew what had to be done. Ten minutes later, someone finally reached through the debris and touched her hand. "Just pull," she said. "I can stand it." At 6:45 A.M., fourteen hours and eight minutes after the furniture store toppled, rescuers gently removed Matkins from the wreckage. When someone took her shoes off, she said, "Don't lose them. They're old but comfortable."

An ambulance rushed Matkins to the hospital, where doctors determined that other than being bruised and exhausted, she had no serious injuries. Twenty-two of her thirty coworkers had been killed.

Matkins was one of 1,223 people treated at local hospitals, 276 of them suffering from major injuries. Only one person died after receiving emergency treatment. All the other fatalities had been killed outright, and many of them remained missing, buried in the mountains of debris covering the core of downtown. Daylight revealed just how devastating the tornado had been. City and state officials estimated property damage at $51 million.

In Bryan the graduate student who had seen the tornado on radar had been up most of the night, watching the eastward progress of the storm system along with fellow researchers and faculty members. As Archie Kahan, director of A&M's Oceanography Department, later wrote, "It was clear that, with a reasonable amount of coordination between existing weather agencies, the means for preventing a large portion of the loss of life in the Waco disaster was at hand but had gone unused."

Had a weather radar warning system been in place, he continued, "the existence of the echoes on the radar scope would have offered a basis for notifying communities in the vicinity of the echoes of the impending danger." Kahan soon drafted a letter proposing that A&M help the state set up such a system.

On June 24 Kahan and others from A&M met with weather bureau officials, representatives of the Texas Department of Public Safety, and other interested parties to discuss what could be done to better warn the public during tornado outbreaks. The meeting and follow-up work resulted in improved communication between the weather bureau and the DPS and marked the beginning of the nation's first weather radar network.

"It was a case of enough is enough," National Weather Service tornado expert Alan Moller later said. "Fifty-three was what broke the camel's back. Since then, not a single tornado in the U.S. has killed more than one hundred people."

In the 1950s meteorologists still relied on simplistic adjectives like "small," "large," and "giant" to describe tornadoes. Based on the review of contemporary accounts and climatological observations, the Waco tornado is now formally classified an F5 on the Fujita Tornado Damage Scale (developed by T. Theodore Fujita at the University of Chicago in 1971). A rating of F5 means that the tornado had wind speeds up to 318 mph, a force sufficient to blow an automobile through the air like a leaf and cause "incredible damage."

By any standard the Waco tornado ranks as the deadliest in Texas history and the tenth-deadliest in the United States. The day it hit, May 11, 1953, also stands as the deadliest single day for tornadoes in Texas. Counting the San Angelo tornado that had struck earlier that day, 125 people died in the violent weather (11 in San Angelo and 114 in Waco). Exactly seventeen years later, a devastating tornado tore through the South Plains city of Lubbock. That storm killed 26 people, for a total May 11 tornado death toll of 151.

In 2003, with the approach of the fiftieth anniversary of the killer storm, Waco civic leaders began an effort to erect a monument remembering the victims. Joe Phipps, the owner of a local monument company, stepped forward to donate the monument and have it installed, a gift amounting to $15,000.

The four-and-a-half-ton, 6-foot-tall, tear-shaped black marble statue lists the names of the 114 Waco storm victims. A contractor from Arlington set the monument in place at Fourth Street and Austin Avenue on August 30, 2004. Another firm donated stone benches for the site, which, at a cost of $98,000, the City of Waco developed as a small park with lights and attractive landscaping.

Roughly 150 people, many of them survivors or relatives of those who died in the storm, gathered for the dedication ceremony on September 2. One of those present was sixty-four-year-old Ed Berry of Fort Worth, whose father, Edward, had been manager of the R. T. Dennis Furniture Store.

"I could hear my mother gasp when she saw the building reduced to a story and a half," Berry recalled at the dedication. "My dad's office was on the mezzanine."

Berry's father and grandfather, Rush Berry, were among the twenty-two people who died inside the store. "There was literally no one left to run the store," he told the newspaper reporter covering the dedication.

Also on hand for the unveiling of the monument was Marlene Fisher. Her father, Irving Ginsburg, died when the tornado destroyed his shop on Austin Avenue, New York Clothiers.

Then sixteen, Fisher had driven downtown that afternoon to pick up her father from work. When she found the downtown streets blocked, she walked the rest of the way to Austin Avenue. "I saw his store demolished," Fisher recalled. "Everybody was just going around in a daze." Back home, she broke the news to her mother that her father was missing. It took another two days before police confirmed that he had been killed.

After all the speeches had been made and photographs taken, Marlene Fisher, Ed Berry, and other survivors lingered at the monument, staring at a line on the memorial taken from a poem by Lord Byron: "Adversity is the path to truth."

RECORD-SETTING SNOWFALL

Panhandle Blizzard

1956

When the *Amarillo Globe-Times* rolled off the press on Wednes-day afternoon, February 1, 1956, the short weather story on page one ran under a two-word headline: "Moisture Skimpy."

In a state stricken with one of the worst droughts in its his-tory, the prospect of only light precipitation from an approach-ing cold front did not come as good news for the Panhandle's ranchers and farmers. Texas desperately needed moisture.

Light snow and freezing drizzle covered most of the area the newspaper called the Golden Spread, but a meteorologist at the local weather bureau said that he did not expect significant accumulations. It would be bitterly cold, with a biting north wind. Weatherman Bob Orion called for a high of only 20 degrees and a low of 7 degrees that night.

When the press run ended, circulation route managers grabbed passing bundles off the conveyor belt and threw the wired squares of newsprint into their trucks. Teenage carri-ers just out of school showed up at collection points across the city to pick up their papers and roll them for home deliv-ery. Larry Todd, a fourteen-year-old Palo Duro High School student, had a 12-block route on Cleveland Street. This thoroughfare intersected one of the most famous highways in America: Route 66.

As Todd tossed the papers from his bicycle, snow continued to fall. When he had covered every house from Northeast Third Street to Fifteenth, he dropped by Ratliff's Drug Store. Normally he ordered a 15-cent cherry-lime drink, but he did not feel like drinking anything cold on this frigid afternoon. Instead, Todd sat at the counter and flipped through the latest issue of *Photoplay* magazine before going home for supper.

All night long the snow came down.

Daylight Thursday revealed a city covered in nearly 2 inches of snow, with precipitation continuing. Todd managed to make it to school, but with icy streets and snowdrifts as high as 2.5 feet in places, absenteeism ran about 25 percent in the city's classrooms.

Residents of Texas's northernmost major city were accustomed to snow and typically took it in stride. Halfway between the state capital in Austin and the Rocky Mountains in Colorado, Amarillo had an average annual snowfall of 16.4 inches. That amount, however, seldom came in just a few days. That Thursday night the weather bureau continued to report that the white stuff would be tapering off, though forecasters expected temperatures to drop as low as 6 degrees below zero in the upper Panhandle.

Snowdrifts began slowing traffic, but city public-works director H. R. Smith said that people still could get where they needed to go, albeit a little slower than usual.

When Thursday's afternoon paper hit the streets, the weather headline had grown to big, bold type, proclaiming: "Storm Closes Many Schools." Even so, the weather bureau predicted that the snow would taper off that afternoon. Precipitation did end about 3 P.M., but by this point Amarillo already had recorded its heaviest snowfall in five years.

At 10:45 A.M. on Friday, February 3, snow again started drifting down on Amarillo and the High Plains. An unusually strong low-pressure system had stalled over the Panhandle just south of Amarillo, pulling in frigid arctic air while sucking Pacific moisture up from Mexico. Not only did this upper-air storm stay put over North Texas, it also grew in power, covering everything below it with wet snow. The weather bureau issued a heavy-snow warning that afternoon. Vicious winds of more than 35 mph added to the misery as the storm worsened into a blizzard.

Snow fell particularly heavily on Plainview, an agricultural town about 70 miles south of Amarillo. By dark, conditions had eroded to the point of crisis. Five miles south of Plainview on U.S. Highway 87, National Guardsmen and Highway Patrol troopers rescued the occupants of a snowbound bus and helped the drivers of thirty stalled vehicles, including the crew of an ambulance that had been rushing a patient with kidney problems from Hale Center to Plainview. Once a wrecker freed the ambulance from the snow, the emergency vehicle finally reached the hospital in Plainview at 8 P.M.

The blizzard worsened. Plainview had nearly a foot of snow on the ground, and it continued to come down. In Amarillo, the weather bureau measured more than 7 inches, with snow still falling. At 7 P.M. on Friday, the city's bus service stopped running. Police urged residents to stay off the streets unless they had an emergency, and city crews fought to keep the major arteries snow free. A few adventurous cabbies, relying on the chains wrapped around their tires, stayed on the streets.

The blizzard paralyzed traffic in the Panhandle for days.
COURTESY *PLAINVIEW DAILY HERALD*

When nurse Beulah Carter's shift at Amarillo's St. Anthony Hospital ended that Saturday morning, only the city's more heavily traveled streets remained passable. A cab driver managed to get Carter within about a half-mile of her house, but he could go no farther.

Believing that she could easily walk the rest of the way home, Carter got out of the cab and began plodding through the snow. She tried to take a shortcut through a lumberyard not far from her residence, but she found it closed. Backtracking to try another route, she stepped into a snowdrift that was deeper than it looked and sunk from sight.

Carter could not get her head up. Struggling in what amounted to cold, white quicksand, she began to think that she would die only 100 yards from the warmth of her small house on Northeast Ninth Street.

Barely able to breathe, Carter frantically began packing snow under her feet to get a better footing. Seconds before she would have lost consciousness from lack of oxygen, she got her head above the snow and carefully worked her way out of the freezing drift. Shivering and exhausted, she made it home.

"I thought that Alaska had moved down on me and sealed me up," she later recalled.

At 9 A.M. on Saturday, Continental Trailways driver John Hearon realized that he would not be pulling into the Tucumcari, New Mexico, bus station on time. After he left Amarillo earlier that morning, driving had become increasingly difficult as the snow on U.S. Highway 66 continued to accumulate. With the bus's windshield wipers doing little to improve visibility in the blowing snow, Hearon drove at only 25 mph. Suddenly, about 63 miles west of Amarillo, the bus hit a deep snowdrift, slowly coming to a stop as the snow filled in over its tires. Despite the driver's best efforts, the bus would not go forward or backward.

Announcing to his sixteen passengers that they would have to wait it out, Hearon kept the diesel engine running so that he could continue to warm the wind-whipped vehicle. He assumed that the bus company's agent in Tucumcari would send help when the bus did not arrive on schedule. Meanwhile, a virtual white hurricane raged outside.

"Along about 2:30 P.M.," Hearon later recalled, "there was still no help in sight and we were running low on fuel. I had used quite a bit trying to get the bus unstuck. I decided the best thing to do was to go for help."

Cautioning his passengers to stay on the bus, Hearon told them that he intended to walk to Glenrio, a small New Mexico town just across the state line, and seek help. Adrian, Texas, would have been a shorter hike, but Hearon knew that it would have been uphill and into the face of a stinging wind.

The thirty-eight-year-old driver made it a couple of miles to the west without too much difficulty, but his legs began to ache from trudging through waist-high snow. And the exertion failed to keep him warm.

"I fell down at least three times but I knew I had to get up and go on," he remembered. "I was afraid to stop because I knew I would never start again." Several times he walked off of the pavement and sank into deeper snow.

With his uniform jacket raised over half of his face to protect him from the icy wind, Hearon struggled on, walking up on several stalled cars and their stranded occupants. One driver beckoned the bus driver to get inside his car for a while to warm up before continuing his trek. Hearon took the man up on his offer but soon pressed on.

Unknown to Hearon, similar scenes played out all across the blizzard-swept Panhandle. Some motorists trapped along farm-to-market roads and major highways risked carbon monoxide poisoning by trying to wait out the storm in vehicles mired in hubcap-deep snow; others trudged to nearby farmhouses or roadside businesses. A Fort Worth & Denver passenger train equipped with a snowplow abandoned its schedule and offered refuge to stranded motorists. Heavy trucks operated by National Guardsmen handled emergency deliveries and medical transport, including a 60-mile round-trip to Washburn to carry a young girl with pneumonia to an Amarillo hospital.

But no vehicles moved on US 66. Hearon's eyes stung constantly from the windblown ice crystals. At some point the driver noticed that he could no longer see out of his right eye.

When the sun set, Hearon's world went from nearly all white to all black. He lost any sense of time, and his left eye began to fail. With the chill factor well below zero, his soaked woolen trouser legs had frozen stiff. Strangely, the icy sheen seemed to protect his body from the wind. His legs felt almost warm. In a lucid moment Hearon realized that he must be suffering from frostbite. Freezing to death, he had heard, was not a bad way to die. After so much cold, you begin to feel warm and comfortable. Then you go to sleep.

But Hearon knew that he could not give up. The lives of his passengers depended on him. He had to keep going though his body cried out for him to stop.

About 11 P.M., eight-and-a-half hours into his trek, the staggering bus driver detected a glare in the distance. "When I saw that light I was too weak to shout very loud for help," he said. "So I started whistling. Someone heard me because three or four men came along and helped me to a gas station."

Glenrio, population less than one hundred, amounted to little more than this combination gas station/bar and a cafe. Hearon sat in exhaustion next to a heater while someone dialed the New Mexico State Police to report a snowbound passenger bus. Even though the bus had stalled in Texas, New Mexico officers began organizing a rescue mission. They drove the 8 miles to the stranded bus and used a large tow truck to pull it out of the snowdrift. By 9 A.M. on Sunday, twenty-four hours after their ordeal began, the vehicle and its passengers arrived safely in Glenrio.

Hearon, meanwhile, had been taken to a hospital in Tucumcari for treatment for shock, frostbite, and temporary snow blindness.

By Sunday night 14 inches of snow covered Amarillo. Farther south, even greater amounts had fallen. Canyon, 30 miles south, had 18 inches on the ground. Hereford, Happy, and Dimmitt each had 24 inches. The heaviest snowfall had hit Plainview, where 29 inches immobilized the town.

Though the blizzard halted almost all transportation in the Panhandle, electric service and the flow of natural gas continued uninterrupted for the most part. As people cooped up in their houses turned to the telephone to keep up with friends and family, the high volume of calls occasionally jammed circuits.

The sun finally broke through the clouds on Monday morning, February 6. "Boy, oh boy, that sun looks good," a reporter for the *Plainview Daily Herald* told the Associated Press bureau in Dallas.

The storm had paralyzed most of the Panhandle and South Plains, but it also killed residents. A Hale County farm woman died in childbirth because she could not get medical treatment in time. When an ambulance finally arrived after a 4-mile trip that took two-and-a-half hours, the driver and his partner found that they were too late. An Amarillo man dropped dead of a heart attack while trying to push his car out of a snowdrift. Another Amarillo man died of an exertion-induced heart attack while shoveling snow.

The Associated Press counted twenty deaths, ranging from weather-related traffic fatalities to cases of exposure and carbon monoxide poisoning, connected to the blizzard. The National Weather Service's Amarillo office later attributed twenty-three deaths to the storm, which sent snow and ice halfway across the state. From an airplane the entire Panhandle looked like a vast Canadian tundra, a brilliant white blanket of snow stretching from horizon to horizon. The snow, beautiful to behold, held the frozen carcasses of thousands of cattle and other livestock.

Knowing that thousands more animals could die unless they got some feed, the agriculture committee of the Amarillo Chamber of Commerce worked with the commander of the Amarillo Air Force Base to arrange an emergency food drop. At 1 P.M. a twin-engine Douglas C-47 loaded with 350 bales of hay took off from the Strategic Air Command facility.

The World War II–era transport flew a low-altitude, 40-mile spiral around Amarillo, the flight crew dropping hay at cattle ranches still isolated by the blizzard. "Operation Haylift," as the military dubbed it, continued for several days.

Despite the heavy loss of livestock, ranchers and farmers gave thanks for the moisture being soaked up by the drought-thirsty soil. Ollie Liner, a Hale County agent for the Texas A&M University Agriculture Extension Service, estimated that the 2-feet-plus snowfall in his county would translate into nearly 2 inches of moisture for the grain fields. Prior to the blizzard, the area had not had any appreciable moisture since October 1955, he said.

The storm would be good for the agriculture community, but it had been bad for business. Stores in Amarillo began opening on a limited basis that Monday, but shelves were sparsely stacked because of the storm's impact on transportation. Trucks, buses, and trains had been unable to get in or out of the Panhandle for days. Supplies of milk and bread had run short in several communities.

After the blizzard stopped blowing, kids in Plainview built this snow dragon.
COURTESY *PLAINVIEW DAILY HERALD*

Panhandle schools finally reopened on February 6, a week after the storm first began producing snow. With some snow-drifts as high as rooftops, snow removal operations continued for another week.

Thirteen months later, another blizzard blew into the Panhandle. Amarillo measured more snow than it had in 1956, and some people argued that the 1957 storm was worse—but National Weather Service records show that memory is selective. With winds gusting to 80 mph, the 1957 blizzard was a nasty storm, but dumped less snow and claimed only half the lives that the previous storm did.

Of Texas's five standing snowfall record categories, the 1956 blizzard still held four of them a half century later: greatest snowfall in a twenty-four-hour period (24 inches in Plainview, February 3 and 4); greatest maximum depth at time of observation (33 inches at Hale Center, south of Plainview in Hale County, February 5); greatest snowfall in a single storm (61 inches at Vega, west of Amarillo in Oldham County, February 1 through 8); and greatest snowfall in one month (61 inches at Vega, February).

Hearon recovered from the effects of his rescue hike, and Continental Trailways awarded him two extra weeks of vacation in recognition of his heroics. Larry Todd kept throwing newspapers for another couple of years, eventually going on to a long career as a radio-television newsman and government public information officer.

"Seldom has our community had to face a crisis such as that over the weekend," the Amarillo newspaper editorialized on February 7. "To call the roll of those who literally put a shoulder to the wheel and kept us all safe and sound would be impossible. . . . No one can really count all the resourceful people who by sheer hard work and devotion averted what could have been tragedy."

BUILDING THE BERMUDA TRIANGLE MYTH

SS *Marine Sulphur Queen* Mystery

1963

After kissing her husband goodbye and watching him walk up the gangway, Mrs. Adam Martin lingered on the dock at Beaumont. The crew of the SS *Marine Sulphur Queen* cast her lines and made ready for sea.

Mrs. Martin could have started her return trip to Austin then, but she stayed on the wharf that day, February 2, 1963, and watched as the molten sulfur–laden tanker slid down the Neches River and headed for the Gulf of Mexico.

"I stood there, alone, watching until she passed out of sight," Mrs. Martin later recalled.

When they left the Capital City to drive to Beaumont, Austin had been basking in an unusual winter heat wave. The temperature reached a record high of 85 degrees that day, and the mercury rose nearly as high on the coast. Now, as Mrs. Martin finally walked back to her car, she felt a strong, cold wind from the north. Winter had returned, leaving the young woman feeling even lonelier.

The Marine Sulphur Queen *after she was refitted to carry molten sulphur.*
COURTESY U.S. COAST GUARD HISTORIAN OFFICE

But her husband, one of the ship's assistant engineers, would be gone for only about two weeks. The *Sulphur Queen* would arrive in Norfolk, Virginia, in five days, pump off its cargo of hot yellow liquid, and dock in Beaumont twelve days after she stood to sea. Rather than return to an empty home, Mrs. Martin drove to Houston to spend a few days with friends before she started a new job at the University of Texas at Austin.

So far as is known, the Texas housewife was the last person to see the 504-foot, 7,240-ton tanker and her crew of thirty-nine men.

The keel of the nineteen-year-old T-2 tanker had been laid in 1944 at the Sun Shipbuilding and Drydock Company in Chester, Pennsylvania. Built for Esso Oil, the ship's original name was the *New Haven*. After World War II she continued to carry oil, but that changed as the chemical industry began to produce new products and look for additional markets.

In 1960 the New York–based Marine Transport Company purchased the *New Haven* and had her refitted at the Bethlehem Steel Company Shipyard in Baltimore to carry liquid sulphur heated to 255 degrees; she was the first vessel of this kind. Renamed the *Marine Sulphur Queen*, the ship got more than a new coat of paint. Her bowels underwent extensive surgery to make room for a 306-foot welded steel tank capable of holding 15,211 long tons of molten sulphur. This insulated, steam-heated tank had been divided into four sulphur-tight compartments to make things more manageable if any leaks occurred. On January 18, 1961, the U.S. Coast Guard certified the *Sulphur Queen* to carry "Grade E liquids at elevated temperatures."

Texas Gulf Sulphur leased the ship. The company had built a large plant outside of Beaumont to extract sulphur from the Spindletop salt dome, site of the state's first gusher in 1901. The company used a technique known as the Frasch process: High-pressure steam was injected into the dome; the steam melted the sulphur below, and the molten element was pumped up into heated tanks. The *Sulphur Queen* was used to transport it. By early 1963 she had made sixty-three trips from Texas to various ports on the eastern seaboard, carrying a substance that could be converted to everything from matches to fertilizer to sulfuric acid.

Beginning her sixty-fourth trip at 6:30 P.M. on February 2, the ship cleared the Sabine sea buoy. After dropping off a pilot who had been onboard, she moved into the open Gulf. As she made to the southeast, the cold front that had roared through Beaumont when Mrs. Martin left the dock picked up speed over the shallow water. Now the north wind gusted well above gale force.

From the bridge Captain James V. Fanning of Beaumont, an experienced master, watched the spray as his ship's 7,200-horsepower, turboelectric power plant pushed her through the increasingly high waves. He knew that the *Sulphur Queen* could easily handle the heavy sea, but the falling barometer told him a rough trip lay ahead, at least until the norther dissipated in the tropics.

Wednesday night, four days after the departure of the *Sulphur Queen*, Mrs. Martin returned to Austin. The next day she started a new job as a Dictaphone operator at the University of Texas. About the time she began wondering what to do for lunch, her brother called.

"Mart's ship is missing," he said.

Thursday night and most of Friday, Mrs. Martin waited confidently for a reassuring telephone call that never came. Surely, she thought, the ship's communication system had failed or the captain had diverted her course because of heavy weather.

On February 8, six days after the ship left Beaumont, the families of those onboard received a telegram similar to the one that came for Mrs. Elaine Vicera of St. Linden, New Jersey:

> Marine Sulphur Queen Scheduled Arrive Norfolk Afternoon 7th Unreported And Overdue Stop Coast Guard And Ships Endeavoring Communicate With And Locate Vessel Stop We Also [sic] Doing Everything Possible And We Will Keep You Closely Advised Marine Transport Lines Inc.

Though only one day overdue, the ship had not been heard from since the early morning hours of February 4. That day at

1:25 A.M. eastern standard time, the Radio Corporation of America's ship-to-shore message center received a buy order from seaman Willie Manuel for his stockbroker in Tampa. The sailor wanted to invest in 5,000 bushels of May wheat. RCA attempted to contact the *Sulphur Queen's* radio operator at 11:23 A.M. with the broker's reply, but it could not raise the vessel.

At the time of Manuel's transmission, the ship reported her position as 26.40 degrees north latitude and 88 degrees west longitude—roughly 200 miles off Key West, Florida. Forty-eight hours from her destination and again at twenty-four hours out, the *Sulphur Queen* should have radioed her position. Neither transmission had been received.

Notified at 9 P.M. EST on February 7 that the *Sulphur Queen* had not arrived as scheduled in Virginia, the Coast Guard made the first of what it called an "All Ships Urgent Broadcast." It sought a response from the *Sulphur Queen* or reports from other vessels of any sighting or radio contact with the overdue ship. The broadcast would continue three times daily.

As of 8 A.M. on February 8, there had been no reply to the morning effort to raise the *Sulphur Queen* by radio. The Coast Guard, with assistance from the U.S. Navy, Marine Corps and Air Force, launched an aerial search of the ship's route from Beaumont to Norfolk, via the Florida Straits.

"I think the *Sulphur Queen* is in Cuba," Mrs. Martin told a reporter for the *Austin Statesman* on February 11. "I've got to believe that. They couldn't have just disappeared, and nobody has reported any wreckage."

The American government certainly would not put anything past Cuban dictator Fidel Castro, whose alliance with Russia still caused great concern. Secret high-altitude spy plane missions checked Cuban ports for any sign that the ship might have been hijacked. The Coast Guard could say publicly only that "other Federal agencies" had checked Cuba "with negative results."

Mrs. Fanning, the captain's wife, remembered the story on page one of the *Beaumont Enterprise* three days after her husband left port. The brutal winter storm that had swept across the Gulf had played havoc with shipping along the east coast of Florida about the time the *Sulphur Queen* would have been riding the bluish green waters of the Gulf Stream through the Florida Straits. Winds gusting to forty-six knots would have churned up mountainous waves nearly 20 feet high.

George W. Simmons, a seaman who had sailed on the *Sulphur Queen* and would have been on her crew this time had he not decided to take the winter off, also suspected the weather. "I think a freak wave hit it," he told a reporter.

The Coast Guard and military search, which covered 30 miles on either side of the ship's estimated course, continued through February 13. The government's effort included eighty-three sorties and covered 348,400 square miles of sea with no results. In addition, forty-two vessels known to have been in the vicinity of the *Sulphur Queen* on February 4 and 5 were contacted to see if they had seen the ship or had any communication with it.

On Valentine's Day the families of *Sulphur Queen* seamen received another telegram, this one from H. L. White, chairman of the board for the Martine Transport Company. He said that the Coast Guard had called off its search for the *Sulphur Queen* and that "present indications indicate probable loss" of the vessel.

Five days later, on February 19, that loss seemed even more certain. A small U.S. Navy vessel operating about 12 miles southwest of Key West sighted some debris bobbing in the water. Moving in for a closer look, the vessel's skipper saw a collection of life jackets and orange life rings.

The first ring fished from the water bore stenciled letters spelling MARINE SULPHUR QUEEN. Before the Naval vessel made for Miami, it retrieved eight life jackets, five life rings, two name boards, a shirt, a piece of oar, an oil can, a gasoline can, a cone buoy, and a foghorn.

The Coast Guard shipped the material to Washington, where an assortment of government experts came to two significant conclusions: Slash marks in two of the life jackets were consistent with an "attack by predatory fish" such as sharks, and the material bore no signs of explosion or fire. Chemical analysis of the shirt did not reveal any trace evidence of sulfur.

Based on the discovery of the flotsam, the Coast Guard mounted a second search from just west of the Dry Tortugas Island to the Bahamas and up the east coast of Florida as far as Cape Canaveral. Seven ships and forty-eight aircraft covered nearly 60,000 square miles of water but found nothing else connected to the *Sulphur Queen*. Navy dive teams also searched unsuccessfully for the ship's hulk.

When nothing else had turned up by March 14, the government again called off its search for the missing Texas-based tanker and its thirty-nine crew members.

"There appears to be no reason for the vessel to have sunk, especially without distress communications," Texas Gulf Sulphur had said in a written statement issued February 14. "The cargo of molten sulphur is not hazardous."

The wives of five ship officers took exception to that. They soon filed a $2.5-million suit in federal district court alleging that the *Sulphur Queen* had been "unsafe, unseaworthy and improperly loaded" when it set sail from Beaumont. The suit further maintained that the tanker had been "carrying an inherently dangerous cargo of liquid sulphur and was not adequately fitted and protected for the carrying of said cargo."

The Coast Guard, meanwhile, convened a board of inquiry in Beaumont on February 20. Along with Texas Gulf and the ship's owners, the board took testimony from an assortment of witnesses. The proceedings later reconvened in New York for additional testimony.

On February 23 a requiem high mass sung at St. Anne's Catholic Church in Beaumont memorialized those lost on the *Sulphur Queen*. Not all of the seamen had been Catholic, but the priest invited "all members of families whose men were on the missing ship, as well as friends of the families." They gained some sense of closure.

More than a month passed.

On April 29 someone came to the Coast Guard station in Corpus Christi with a note written with a ballpoint pen on a piece of paper that looked like it could have been torn from a grocery bag. The man said that he had found the note in a bottle floating in the Laguna Madre, the long bay between the mainland and Padre Island. Unsigned, the note referred to an explosion with two men hurt. The writer also had sketched a crude map of the Gulf, with a circled X and the word SHIP near the western approach to the Florida Straits.

Investigators never determined whether the note was genuine. The FBI crime laboratory concluded that the note had been written by a particular crew member, but the U.S. Coast and Geodetic Survey said that a bottle dropped in the water off Key West was not likely to have drifted to the Corpus Christi area unless a strong southwesterly wind had blown several days before and after it was dropped.

A year after the *Sulphur Queen*'s disappearance, an article in the February 1964 issue of the popular men's magazine *Argosy* added a new landmark to the geography of world imagination: the Bermuda Triangle. In an article entitled "The Deadly Bermuda Triangle," writer Vincent Gaddis described a mysterious triangle with apexes at Bermuda; Miami, Florida; and San Juan, Puerto Rico. Inside that area, he wrote, an unusually high number of boats, ships, and airplanes had inexplicably disappeared over the years.

The most recent of those disappearances was the *Sulphur Queen*. Gaddis's later inclusion of the Bermuda Triangle story in his book *Invisible Horizons: True Mysteries of the Sea,* ensured a new myth's lasting place in popular culture.

The Bermuda Triangle makes for good stories, but the only scientific fact that distinguishes the area is that it is one of two places on earth where a magnetic compass points to due north rather than magnetic north. Unless a compass is adjusted for this variation, serious navigation errors can occur. Beyond that, as the Coast Guard says in a Bermuda Triangle fact sheet available on its Web site, "The Coast Guard is not impressed with supernatural explanations of disasters at sea. It has been their experience that the combined forces of nature and unpredictability of mankind outdo even the most far fetched science fiction many times each year."

The consolidated wrongful-death lawsuits filed by families of the missing officers and crew dragged on in the federal court system until 1972. Eventually, the plaintiffs received a multimillion-dollar settlement, with the U.S. Court of Appeals, Second Circuit, ruling that the claimants had "sustained their burden of proving [the *Sulphur Queen's*] unseaworthiness" due primarily to the heavy load that it had carried.

In January 2001 scuba divers with the Association of Underwater Explorers investigated a large metallic hulk resting upside-down in 423 feet of water about 140 miles out in the Gulf of Mexico from Fort Myers, Florida. Onboard one of the two support vessels was the daughter of a *Sulphur Queen* officer. Though divers found no conclusive evidence as to the identity of the ship, they could not rule out that the wreck was the *Sulphur Queen*. Until the hulk of the *Sulphur Queen* is positively identified, the mystery of its disappearance will endure.

CHAPTER 17

FLASH FLOOD

Tragedy in Terrell County
1965

When the ringing telephone jarred Terrell County Sheriff Bill Cooksey from an exhausted sleep early that morning, he knew it meant trouble.

"Hey, She'ff, your town's washing away," Border Patrolman Kenneth Epperson yelled into the phone in his heavy Cajun accent.

Cooksey, Epperson, Sanderson Volunteer Fire Chief Buddy Sudduth, and others had been up until nearly 4 A.M. training spotlights on the chocolate-colored water roaring down Sanderson Creek on the south side of Sanderson, a West Texas town of 2,300. It had started raining heavily over the mountains west of town about 8 P.M. that Thursday, June 10, 1965. The rain continued off and on through the night, the runoff sending a significant rise down the normally dry creek. As much as 6 inches of rain had fallen, but the precipitation finally tapered off early Friday morning.

The sheriff had been poised to order an evacuation of the lower part of town, but when the water began to recede, the officers had gone to their homes for some badly needed rest.

As they slept a giant mass of disturbed air recharged itself over the canyon extending 33 miles above the town and began moving east. About 5 A.M. on Friday, June 11, it started raining again—torrentially. By daybreak water in the creek ran higher than it had the night before, and it continued to rise.

Epperson had been awakened somewhere between 6 and 6:30 A.M. by incessant honking outside his house. Ready to jump down someone's throat for waking him up so soon after a very long night, he looked outside to see who was sitting on his horn at that time of the morning. First he noticed that water covered his yard. Then the border patrolman recognized James Albert Mansfield standing on a butane tank that was rapidly disappearing in rising water. Epperson later learned that Mansfield had seen the rising water and driven through the south end of Sanderson, blowing his truck's horn to warn residents. Just before the water forced him to abandon his pickup truck, Mansfield's Paul Revere efforts had jarred Epperson into consciousness.

The border patrolman awakened his family, dressed quickly, and drove his wife and daughter to Harvey's Cafe on Main Street, the town's social center. From there, having seen firsthand that Mansfield was not exaggerating the situation, he telephoned the sheriff.

A former highway patrolman, Cooksey had been sheriff since 1961. He and his chief deputy had 1,257 square miles of county to cover, including the unincorporated county-seat town of Sanderson. On that day, unfortunately, Chief Deputy Dalton Hogg was on vacation in Louisiana.

As Cooksey headed toward Harvey's to gulp down some desperately needed coffee, Epperson drove his government jeep back to his house to rescue a kitten that his thirteen-year-old daughter had recently found. He succeeded in saving the cat but did not have time to gather up anything else. A wave of water soon swept through his small redbrick house, scattering his family's possessions, including his badge and gun.

Leaving Harvey's, Cooksey splashed through water above his boot tops to get back to his county vehicle, a station wagon that doubled as the county's ambulance. By this point Fire Chief Sudduth had warned the managers of Sanderson's motels, all located on U.S. Highway 90 in the southern part of town, that their places of business likely would be flooded.

The busy highway, Sanderson's main thoroughfare, was the nation's southernmost route from Florida to California. About a block south of that roadway lay the mainline of the transcontinental Southern Pacific Railroad. Transportation, in fact, was Sanderson's reason for being. First known as Straw-bridge, the town had been developed when the railroad came through in 1881. The railroad maintained a rail yard and repair facility in town, and eight train crews lived there. In all, the SP had about 150 employees in Sanderson; this business, along with sheep and goat ranching, constituted the mainstay of the local economy.

Joe Fuentes, who worked at the SP depot, saw the rising water on his way to work. Like Mansfield, he began driving through town with his fist on the horn, trying to warn those living in low-lying areas.

Old-timers remembered that Sanderson Creek had flooded three times before back in the 1930s. Each time, despite big rains, the high water had receded almost as fast as it had gone up. This morning, even though the creek seemed to be getting deeper and wider by the minute, no one felt overly concerned. They were sure that the water would go down as soon as the rain stopped. But the water continued to rise.

Cooksey and others who had been around for a while certainly understood the dynamics of the situation. The long canyon extended uphill from the community, with Sanderson Creek cutting through the southern part of town. Any time it rained heavily to the west of town, the runoff found its way down scores of steep ravines, including a major feature known as Three-Mile Draw, and then poured down Sanderson Canyon. Eventually the runoff made its way to the Rio Grande.

But on this summer morning in 1965, the runoff came higher and faster than anyone had ever seen. Unknown to the sheriff and other residents of the town, a rooftop-high wall of water surged down the canyon straight for Sanderson.

Around 7 A.M. someone called Frances Corbett and told her to get out of her house. "The creek is running full and the water is lapping over the bridge," the caller warned. Looking outside, Corbett saw her yard already covered with water. She woke up her five children and told them that they needed to get dressed. As soon as she could, she herded them into the family station wagon and drove toward town.

She made it only 1 block before she saw what looked like a tidal wave of biblical proportions headed their way. The family barely made it to higher ground before the water roared by.

Judging by the time frozen on all of the clocks that stopped when the electric lines went down, the flood crest hit Sanderson at 7:05 A.M. that Friday. Hydrologists later estimated that water roared down the creek at a rate of 76,415 cubic feet per second.

A trio of 1,000-pound metal gasoline tanks bobbed down the creek like loose fishing corks. Telephone poles that had washed out of the rocky ground penetrated the reinforced steel walls of the Sanderson Wool Commission Company warehouse like pencils poking through cardboard.

Reaching the main line of the Southern Pacific, the water ripped up track and swept away railroad cars like they were toys. As the water approached the train yard, SP porter A. F. Scott barely had time to climb up on an old passenger car he used as living quarters. Soon the rail car, with Scott clinging to the top, floated downstream.

County Judge R. S. Wilkinson and his wife watched the unfolding disaster from the roof of their one-story home. As the railroad car floated by, Wilkinson yelled at Scott to grab the telephone lines as he passed under them. But no one could hear anything over the roar of the raging water.

Morris Nichols, a twenty-two-year-old SP brakeman, had spent the night at Robertson's Motel, an old-style tourist court on US 90. The rain woke him around 5 A.M., but he did not have much trouble falling back asleep. Nichols managed to get in another two hours of shut-eye before the rapidly rising floodwater suddenly broke open the door to his room. The startled railroad man pulled on his pants and then sloshed through the water to the room next door, where John Johnson and his family were staying.

"Let's get your kids out of here," Nichols yelled. "There's a flood coming."

By now the water came up to his chest. Nichols said that he would take three of Johnson's kids and head for higher ground, but the rushing water prevented Johnson from being able to get the door open.

Johnson yelled for Nichols to go around to the back of the cabin. Nichols swam most of the way behind the motel, but before he could get to the Johnsons' room, the flood crest crashed into the motel. The water surged over Nichols's head, but he fought his way to the surface.

"I tried to get on the roof of the motel," he later told the Associated Press, "but I couldn't pull myself up. Finally I turned loose. I thought I was going to die."

The current swept Nichols about 300 feet before he managed to grab onto a telephone pole. Then a car floated up, pinning him against the pole.

"I looked back and saw all the Johnson kids up on top of the motel," Nichols continued. "John had put them up on the roof through a back window."

As Nichols watched helplessly, the motel began to break up from the relentless pounding of the debris-laden floodwater. Then it turned over in the water and everyone who had been on the roof disappeared. A few moments later, the water rose over his head again and Nichols had to let go of the sturdy pole and take his chances in the current.

The water swept him another quarter of a mile downstream before he felt the ground under his feet. Staggering out of the water to higher ground, he recognized the bodies of two of the Johnson children.

Dazed, exhausted, and bleeding from numerous cuts, Nichols sat down and did the only thing he could think to do: He prayed. After a while he got up, but he did not know where he was going when he walked away.

"When it was all over," he went on, "I just walked and walked. It was like a dream—a bad dream seeing those children dying like that and you can't do anything about it."

Eight days before, on June 3, astronaut Edward White II had exited his Gemini 4 capsule for mankind's first "walk" in space. He stayed outside the capsule twenty-two minutes as Americans and the rest of the free world listened to live radio transmissions from him and mission control. Sanderson seemed that remote on June 11—but it had no communication with the outside world. The phone lines were down. Fast-moving water still covered the two highways leading out of town. Sheriff Cooksey could radio his office from his county vehicle, but the small department's base station could not even cover every corner of Terrell County.

As Cooksey and other officers began recovering bodies, Epperson recalled that he had seen a private airplane undergoing a paint job at a local shop. The border patrolman had a pilot's license and assumed that he could fly the plane to Fort Stockton, the closest town, and let the rest of Texas know that Sanderson needed help. The idea was sound, but the torrential rains had soaked the plane's magneto. He could not get it started.

Jolly Harkins, the postmaster, remembered that his wife had an old shortwave radio gathering dust in their garage. Unfortunately, they did not know how to use it. Cooksey finally located someone, SP employee Phillip Hanson, who thought that he could get the transmitter working. Bill Ray of the U.S. Soil and Conservation Service brought in a portable generator to power the set.

As soon as the tubes warmed up, Hanson spoke into the microphone. "May-day, May-day. . . . Sanderson has been hit by a flash flood," he said repeatedly. "May-day, May-day. . . . We need assistance."

The set's receiver did not work, so no one knew for sure whether it was putting out a signal. Fortunately, it was. A communications operator at the Naval Air Station in Kingsville,

Texas—some 430 miles from Sanderson—monitored the repetitive transmissions and contacted the Texas Department of Public Safety communications center in Pecos and the Reeves County sheriff's office in Fort Stockton. Not knowing that the radio had done its job, Hanson kept up his repeated call for help.

Around midmorning Cooksey heard an airplane circling overhead. That, he realized, meant that the outside world finally had become aware of the situation in Sanderson.

Help began arriving by noon. The DPS sent every available highway patrolman in West Texas and started a portable communication bus rolling from Austin. Sheriffs and deputies from other counties arrived to volunteer their services. The Border Patrol dispatched agents to lend a hand. Soon the American Red Cross and Salvation Army had personnel in Sanderson.

The immediate problem was finding those who were missing, including the guests at Robertson's Motel. In addition to Johnson, his wife Ethel, and their six children, the four children of Mr. and Mrs. Felix Sellers also were missing from the destroyed motel. Searchers finally found twelve-year-old Michael Johnson wandering well downstream from the washed-out lodgings. In shock, he could hardly speak. Cooksey soon realized why: The youngster had just seen his entire family wash down the creek. As soon as the highway became passable, a volunteer drove the boy to the hospital at Fort Stockton. Later, someone had to tell him that he was the only one in his family who had survived.

The rain had stopped and the floodwaters had receded, but nature was giving Sanderson no break. That afternoon the temperature rose above 100 degrees. The thinner layers of mud dried quickly, and before the sun set, blowing dust made conditions miserable for searchers and other relief workers.

The flash flood in Sanderson washed out U.S. Highway 90, then a major east–west artery.   COURTESY TEXAS DEPARTMENT OF TRANSPORTATION

Sixteen bodies had been recovered by Monday afternoon, three days after the flood. One by one, the other victims were found along the Rio Grande, bringing the death toll to twenty-six. The body of the railroad porter, A. F. Scott, was found near Eagle Pass. The last victim, a child, was found 300 miles downriver in Nuevo Laredo, Mexico. The bodies of two victims, John Johnson and Jesus Marguez, were never discovered.

In addition to the lives it claimed, the flash flood destroyed 54 homes and partially damaged another 169 residences. In all, 450 Sanderson residents had been displaced by the disaster. Several businesses also were destroyed, including Robertson's Motel, the Clymer Courts, the Sunset Siesta Motel, the Kerr Mercantile Company warehouse, and the wool commission warehouse. Beyond the damage to the latter building, the flood scattered thousands of dollars worth of mohair for miles downstream; the white wool clinging to the thorny brush looked like snow.

The Sanderson Bank, Oasis Restaurant, Western Hills Motel, Dairy King, and the post office also sustained major damage in the flood. Officials estimated that the property damage would reach $1.6 million.

The disaster hurt Sanderson in another poignant way: Floodwaters had ripped through two of the town's cemeteries, moving grave markers and washing away bodies and bones. Unidentified remains, to the sorrow of surviving family members, had to be reburied in a mass grave.

Sanderson recovered from the flood, but in later years several economic factors proved nearly as devastating. The completion of Interstate 10 in the early 1980s took much of the cross-country traffic away from US 90, and the railroad shut down its Sanderson yard. By the 2000 census the population of Sanderson had dropped nearly 60 percent from its 1965 level.

But those who still live there are much safer from floods than they used to be. Starting in 1969, four years after the disaster, the U.S. Soil and Conservation Service completed a fifty-page study calling for construction of eleven flood-control dams along Sanderson Canyon. After that, land acquisition and environmental studies took another nine years.

Finally, thirteen years after the flood, construction of the first dam began in 1978. By the time the last dam was completed in 1987, a project with an estimated 1969 price tag of $4.6 million ended up costing taxpayers $34 million. People joked that it would have been cheaper for the government to just move the town, but nothing like the tragedy that devastated Sanderson in the summer of 1965 is likely to ever happen again.

TERRIBLE TUESDAY

Wichita Falls Tornado
1979

It was a typical day in Wichita Falls, a northwest Texas town of almost 100,000 residents. Sheppard Air Force Base began another day training the next generation of jet pilots. Students at Midwestern State University showed up for classes and looked forward to the end of the spring semester. Baseball fans anticipated the start of the Major League season that night and hoped that those perennial losers, the Texas Rangers, would have a successful debut in their season opener at Arlington against the Cleveland Indians. Thousands of men and women who worked in oil-processing and agricultural businesses, the lifeblood Wichita Falls, started another day of work. And the crew at the Western Sizzlin' steakhouse opened for another day of feeding the hundreds of hungry patrons who flocked to the restaurant for its meat and potatoes fare.

By all accounts, Tuesday, April 10, 1979, was just another day. But when it was over, those who survived the day would never forget it, even if they tried. It changed Wichita Falls forever. Many say for the better.

The people of Wichita Falls did not know it, but hundreds of miles away in Kansas City, meteorologists at the National Weather Service's Severe Storms Forecast Center were becoming worried. Their apprehension grew as the morning progressed. Satellite and radar images and the flow of data on air masses, temperatures, dew points, and winds that they received from weather-monitoring devices continued to indicate a worsening threat of thunderstorms and tornadoes. By noon the scientists realized that the threat was real. They only had to predict how soon the storms would develop and estimate the size of the at-risk area.

At 1:55 P.M. the Severe Storms Forecast Center issued Tornado Watch Number 67, warning of the possibility of tornadoes, large hail, and damaging thunderstorm winds across a 30,000-square-mile area in North-Central Texas and southwestern Oklahoma, including Wichita County and Wichita Falls. National Weather Service offices in Fort Worth and Oklahoma City flashed the statement to the threatened area, and local radio and television stations broadcast it. Storm-spotter networks were activated, sending men and women with two-way radios in their cars and pickup trucks across the area to provide an early warning if dangerous weather developed.

In Wichita Falls the warning was noted, and, as with any severe weather alert, some people took it more seriously than others. For the most part, Wichitans felt no great concern. After all, it was spring in Tornado Alley. Severe weather watches were not uncommon in March, April, and May as the cold air of a dying winter and the warming air of an approaching summer clashed in an often explosive struggle for supremacy. And Wichita Falls, named for the Wichita Indians who lived near waterfalls on what is now the Wichita River, was no stranger to tornadoes. On March 31, 1958, one man was killed when a twister leveled the community of Dean, just east of town; and on April 3, 1964, a tornado ripped across the northwest part of Wichita Falls and through Sheppard Air Force Base, killing seven people and injuring sixty-nine others. Many smaller storms had raked the area, but it had been fifteen years since there had been a major tornado, and memories tend to dim with time.

By midafternoon, as the Texas sun sent temperatures climbing, storms began developing to the west and moving east. Local law enforcement authorities went on alert, with police officers patrolling the edges of the city ordered to keep a close eye on the skies.

And then spring unleashed its fury. The town of Vernon, 56 miles northwest of Wichita Falls, got hit first. Just before 3:30 P.M. a tornado slashed through the city. It killed 13 of the Vernon's 11,000 residents, injured several more, destroyed more than one hundred homes, and caused property damage estimated at $20 million.

Rescue workers and news reporters descended on Vernon. The bodies of the victims were collected, and the injured were loaded into ambulances for transport to the hospitals in Wichita Falls. This, everyone figured, was what the weather forecasters had warned them about. They had no idea that even worse was yet to come in just a couple of hours.

As the weather continued to deteriorate and news of the Vernon disaster was broadcast across Wichita Falls, police officers Nick Neuberth, Bruce Stanford, Bill Horton, and David Terronez were sent to Memorial Stadium, the high school football field in the southwest corner of town, to act as storm spotters. Meanwhile, fry cook Larry Jones reported for work at the

The Witchita Falls tornado of 1979 in "mature" stage.
PHOTO BY D. BURGESS, COURTESY NOAA PHOTO LIBRARY, NOAA CENTRAL LIBRARY;
OAR/ERL/NATIONAL SEVERE STORMS LABORATORY (NSSL)

Western Sizzlin' on Kemp Boulevard about 5 P.M. A worried coworker, Rene Graves, asked him if he would protect her if a tornado came their way. Nothing like that is going to happen, he assured her, but if it did, sure, he would protect her from harm. They laughed it off and went back to work.

As the work day ended, most people headed home for dinner and a night of television. As the 5:30 P.M. *CBS Evening News* neared an end, Walter Cronkite read a news bulletin about the Vernon tornado. Little did those watching know that the next day Cronkite would be talking about their city.

Just before 6 P.M. a monstrous black cloud dropped from the skies on the south side of town and began its death march across the defenseless city. "The giant tornado was a massive black column extending from the low striated base of the inky clouds to the ground," a National Weather Service report later said. "Huge pieces of debris thrown high in the air were clearly visible from miles away as the storm cut a swath of destruction through the city. Eyewitnesses described details of the storm differently, but they were unanimous on one point—it was an awesome, terrifying experience beyond anything they had encountered before."

The police officers at Memorial Stadium could attest to that. They watched in horror from outside the stadium press box as the cloud—containing at least five funnels—moved straight toward them. Knowing that they could not outrun it, they bolted down the stadium stairs, huddled against a steel stairway railing, locked their arms together, and prayed. One of them later told a reporter that he just prayed his body could be identified. The roar of the storm was deafening, and the group was blasted by swirling debris.

But then the roar stopped. The mile-wide tornado moved on, looking for more victims, and the police officers were alive. The winds had torn the speakers from their radios, their hand-cuffs had been sucked out of their leather cases, and even their service revolvers had been ripped open. Neuberth's watch had stopped at 6:05 P.M.

The police officers were not the only ones trying to strike a bargain with God that day. At the Western Sizzlin' the manager warned other employees and customers that a tornado was coming. They all huddled together on their knees, with their hands over their heads, near the restaurant kitchen's massive walk-in refrigerator.

"The lights went out," Jones later wrote in twentieth-anniversary remembrance of the storm for the *Wichita Falls Times Record News.*

I believe everyone was praying at that time. I heard Rene holler out my name, "Larry." It was pitch black, so I told her, "Rene, keep yelling out my name and hold out your hand and I will find you." I walked through the blackness and found her hand . . . I sat down on my knees behind her and covered her up. I coupled my hands overhead and tried to save her as she had requested about an hour earlier.

The tornado swallowed the restaurant and turned it into a pile of junk in a matter of seconds. Jones recalled the aftermath:

I felt debris hitting me in the back. It felt like I got shot in the back with a shotgun. I guess it was glass, sand and small debris because it stung real bad. Then I missed out on time somehow because it was over as fast as it came and I was face down in the dining area on the carpet. I was lying over a stainless steel rack that was about two feet wide, like a plus sign. It was on the carpet and I was on top of it. It went across my legs and my stomach.

There was a block wall that had ceramic tile on one side of it on top of me. I screamed out for help, and the wall settled down on me and pushed my stomach down on the angle edge of the rack. I then started suffocating. I could not get one ounce of air, so I started praying silently and crying out to God. "God, if you will save me, I will serve you forever." Then I blacked out as if I was dead.

Jones came to as someone pulled him from the rubble. Although suffering from a crushed stomach and intestines and other internal injuries that would require major surgery, he struggled to his feet and slumped in a chair. That's when he heard a woman's anguished scream: "She's dead, oh my God. She's dead." He knew that the woman was talking about Rene. Jones stood up and vomited. He had not been able to keep his promise to her.

At the Sikes Senter mall, the town's major shopping venue, a deadly drama unfolded. Panicked shoppers, ignoring frantic pleas to stay inside, rushed to their cars to flee. Many did not make it. When the tornado swept across the mall, seven people died and dozens were injured as their cars were crushed or hurled across the parking lot. One witness watched horror-struck as the wind slammed a car door on a woman's leg so violently that it severed the lower portion of the limb, sucking it up into the clouds. No one who stayed inside the mall had been injured. The tornado demonstrated the folly of trying to outrun a twister in a car. Twenty-five of the storm's victims died in their cars and thirty of the fifty-nine most seriously injured people were hurt in their cars or trucks.

Gwen Lazenby had just gotten off work and arrived at her trailer home on Windthorst Road when a TV news bulletin told her that a tornado was on the ground. She immediately called her mother.

"As I was talking to her, I opened the front door to see what the noise was that I was hearing," she wrote in her remembrance for the *Times Record News*.

As I looked out my front door, I saw nothing but solid black and debris flying all around only two blocks in front of me. I yelled to mother on the phone: "My God, we're gonna get hit!" She yelled at me to get the girls and go get under the bed. I grabbed the girls, went to the bedroom and got under the bed. Before I could say a prayer, the tornado hit us.

The tornado lifted our trailer house up off its foundation, took it up in the air with it, turned us over and over, carried us about $^1/_2$ to $^3/_4$ mile away from the park, then the
trailer exploded, and the girls and I fell to the ground. The
trailer and all of our belongings were blown to who knows
where, but the girls and I fell within six feet of each other in
a field. When I woke up, it was raining.

As I looked around, I saw my oldest daughter. Her leg
looked as though it was not part of her body. It was twisted
back. Then I heard my youngest daughter crying. I turned
and called for her. She looked like she was OK, except for
some cuts and bruises. I tried to get up and walk, but I
noticed I had a fractured ankle, I also received a broken
pelvis, and had a bedspring wire about 2 feet long in my
head. It had entered through the left eyelid and [was] pro-
truding out the side of my head. My oldest daughter told me
to pull it out. I feared I might be going blind. I started
yelling, and the girls joined in.

Their screams attracted rescuers, and they were taken to
the hospital. When they were released, the Federal Emergency
Management Agency put them up temporarily in a new
home—a damaged trailer.

The storm, later determined to be an F4 on the Fujita Tornado Damage Scale, roared across the city with winds as high
as 260 mph. People sought shelter wherever they could. They
cowered in refrigerator vaults, closets, stairwells, bathtubs,
even a bank vault. Then, after almost an hour of dealing death
and destruction along a 47-mile path across Wichita Falls and
into Oklahoma, the tornado dissipated. In its wake forty-two
people were dead, with more than 1,700 others swamping the

Wichita General and Bethania Hospitals seeking treatment. A large portion of the city lay devastated. Some 5,000 homes and businesses had been destroyed, and more than 20,000 people—almost a fifth of the city's population—were left homeless.

North Texas and southern Oklahoma were battered with thirteen tornadoes in a four-hour span that day. In all, 53 people died and more than 1,900 suffered injuries. Property losses totaled more than $63 million.

"The three main storms in the Red River Valley outbreak were giant tornadoes," the weather-service report said. "Each lasted for an hour or more and left a continuous track of ground damage 35 miles or longer. In addition, the damage paths of all three were wider than normal. This was especially true of the Wichita Falls tornado, whose more than 1-mile-wide path of damage is one of the biggest on record."

Rescue and relief workers from across the state rushed to Wichita Falls after the storm and began picking through tangled mountains of debris in a desperate search for the dead and injured. Help came from all quarters. Armies of physicians and other medical personnel, utility repair crews, and construction workers moved in to treat the injured and rebuild the shattered city. Haggar Slacks donated clothes to people who had lost all their apparel. Country singer Jimmy Dean sent a truckload of his sausage to help feed the homeless.

Tornado researchers also came to Wichita Falls. They noticed that often in the midst of the debris, a small closet or bathroom would be untouched. What they learned ultimately led to the development of "safe rooms," center rooms with reinforced walls that can protect people during storms. The Federal Emergency Management Agency (FEMA) now includes building plans and information about safe rooms in its brochures.

Aerial view of the damage in Witchita Falls on April 12, 1979.
NOAA PHOTO

After the initial shock wore off and workers had hauled away all the debris, Wichita Falls began rebuilding. Spurred by its motto, "The City That Faith Built," the city undertook an ambitious civic improvement plan known as Goals for Wichita Falls. It included a comprehensive economic development plan; land-use management control; improved education facilities; increased funding for street maintenance, parks, and other recreation areas; and flood-control projects. Just two years after the storm, the National League of Cities recognized the city's renaissance and named Wichita Falls an All-American city.

Banker Gail Natale, who survived her home being shredded by the storm, told the *Times Record News,* "The folks here, we'd always been known for living in Tornado Alley. All of a sudden, we were proud of what a town could do. There was just real pride in being here."

"HORIZONTAL TORNADOES"

The Crash of Delta 191
1985

Johnny Meier, a frequent airline passenger, had his own preflight checklist. The thirty-five-year-old Texan always did two things before flying commercially: He insisted on a window seat, and just before takeoff he said a short, silent prayer.

On Friday afternoon, August 2, 1985, Meier waited at a Delta Airlines gate at the Fort Lauderdale–Hollywood International Airport in Florida for a 1,115-mile flight to Dallas. After a two-hour layover at Dallas–Fort Worth International Airport, known by most travelers simply as DFW, he would catch a commuter flight for Killeen. From there he had only a short drive to his home in Temple.

When the ticket agent announced that Flight 191 could be boarded, Meier checked his seat number—41J—and moved down the walkway to the plane. Taking his seat next to the window, he settled down for the flight back to Texas. As district manager for a wholesale grocery chain, Meier had been in Florida for two weeks developing a new delivery route. A coworker had proposed that they travel back to Texas together on a flight through Atlanta, but Meier declined. He wanted to get home, and the Fort Lauderdale–to–Los Angeles flight, with its one stop in Dallas, was the quickest way for him to get there.

At 4:10 P.M. eastern time, the Lockheed L1011 Tri-Star departed Florida on time. The jumbo jet, referred to by air-traffic controllers as a "heavy," could hold 302 passengers. But that day the plane departed with only half that number—152 passengers and 11 crew members.

As soon as the FASTEN SEATBELT light went off, the flight attendants began working their way up and down the aisle, offering drinks. Dinner would follow. Meier ordered a soft drink—he never drank alcohol when he flew—to go with his roast beef sandwich.

The two-hour and thirty-two-minute flight proceeded routinely until Captain Edward Connors flipped on the loud-speaker and announced that he had made a change in course that would delay their arrival a bit. He had opted to fly farther north to avoid a developing area of stormy weather along the Texas-Louisiana coastline. Now over northeast Texas, he told his passengers that he would have to circle Texarkana, a city half in Texas and half in Arkansas, until he could get clearance into DFW. The weather had backed up air traffic, but Connors estimated that they would be at the gate only ten or fifteen minutes late. Apologizing for that inconvenience, the captain promised to be a good tour guide and point out interesting features below.

Glad that the pilot did not want to take any chances, Meier thought about his family. They lived only 3 miles from the air-port, and his wife often brought the kids there to meet him when he got off the plane. He hoped that she had decided to do that this evening. He also hoped that he could work in a little time on the golf course over the weekend.

Finally cleared to head toward Dallas, Captain Connors left his orbit over Texarkana. In Stephenville, a town about 100 miles southwest of the Fort Worth–Dallas area, National Weather Service radar technician Ruben Encinas realized he needed supper. At 5:30 P.M. he checked the scope and saw nothing unusual. Ten minutes later he walked into a nearby break room to eat.

Devoting only eight minutes to his meal, Encinas took an atmospheric reading at 5:48 P.M. Returning to his radar at 6 P.M., he noted that conditions in North Texas had changed. In the half hour that he had been gone from the screen, a sudden heat-generated thunderstorm had developed over DFW.

Now approaching DFW at 10,000 feet, Connors observed a "pretty good size" thunderstorm and asked the flight controller to let him go around it. The captain requested a new heading, got permission from a flight controller to take it, and moved around the cell.

At 5:56 P.M. the tower alerted all aircraft of "a little rainshower just north of the airport" and told pilots to tune to the frequency needed for an instrument landing on runway 17-L. Eyeing the shower, Connors asked for a 20-degree course change to avoid the weather. The tower approved. But now the captain saw that the thunderstorm roiled right on top of the runway his jet was approaching at 170 knots.

"We're gonna get our airplane washed," First Officer Rudolph Price said to Connors.

"What?" Connors asked.

"We're gonna get our airplane washed," Price repeated.

Back in his seat, Meier did not need radar to tell him that the jet would be landing in the rain. To the right of the airplane, all Meier could see was black. He knew that they were probably in for a bumpy arrival.

Now only a little more than 4 miles from the airport, Delta 191 had three planes lined up to land ahead of it. At fifty-four seconds past 6 P.M., as Connors and his copilot moved through their routine approach procedures, Meier and the other passengers in the plane felt the jet's landing gear begin to go down.

On the ground, the copilot of another Delta flight that had just landed remarked to his captain: "Is that a waterspout out there on the end [of the runway]?" The pilot replied: "I don't know. Sure looks like it, doesn't it. Looks like a tornado or something. I've never seen anything like it."

But the rain obscured the view from Flight 191, which continued its approach at an airspeed of 160 knots. "Tower," Connor radioed. "Delta 191 heavy. Out here in the rain. Feels good."

At 6:04 P.M. the tower cleared the jet for landing. Eighteen seconds later, with the plane at about 1,500 feet, Price saw lightning and told the captain.

"Where?" Connors asked.

"Right ahead of us," Price replied.

From his seat Meier could not see the lightning, but horizontal streaks of water ran across his window as the plane flew through the thunderstorm. Despite the weather, Meier could see Lake Grapevine below. The woman sitting behind him was getting antsy. "Don't worry about it," Meier told her. "There won't be a problem. Planes always take off and land in the rain."

Up in the cockpit, Connors had a hard time believing his airspeed indicator. His copilot had throttled back to 150 knots, but the jet's airspeed was rising, peaking at a little more than 173 knots. Checking the altimeter, Connors saw that the plane was now only 800 feet above the ground.

"Watch your speed," Connors said to Price, apparently thinking that the First Officer had moved the throttle forward.

With rain pounding the aluminum fuselage, Connors was beginning to realize that they were caught up in the turbulent winds of the thunderstorm. He warned Price to watch for a sudden drop in airspeed. To compensate for that, the copilot pushed the throttles to send more fuel to the plane's three powerful Rolls Royce jet engines. The plane's nose went up as if the aircraft were about to climb, but the instruments showed that it was continuing to lose both altitude and airspeed. In fact, the big jet was getting dangerously close to the speed at which it would no longer fly—what aviators call "stall speed."

For a moment the jet seemed to normalize, with the airspeed picking up, albeit slowly. Then, only 635 feet up, the plane's airspeed plummeted twenty knots in one second. Suddenly the jet rolled to the left, with the wing on that side tipping downward by 20 degrees.

"Hang on to the son of a bitch!" the captain shouted to Price.

In the main cabin, the passengers realized that the plane definitely was in trouble. Some of them began to cry while others, including flight attendant Wendy Robinson, began to pray.

On the flight deck, the Ground Proximity Warning System went off, its mechanical voice saying, "Pull up!" Connors made that an order to Price. "Toga," he yelled, aviation shorthand for "take off, go around." But the copilot could not coax any airspeed out of the plane's engines.

Like many people faced with death, Meier refused to think that he might be about to die. Surely the plane would make it, just like all of the planes he had flown in the past. Looking out the window, he saw grass below.

Now fully at the mercy of the savage downdrafts caused by the thunderstorm, the jet briefly came down on its belly in a field, immediately bouncing back into the air. Traveling at 1,700 feet a minute, the airliner roared over pavement.

Meier saw a hard surface just below his window and thought that the plane had made it over the runway. But what he saw was not an airport runway. It was State Highway 114.

The highway cut a wide, inverted V through the northern edge of DFW. Now that the worst of rush hour had died down, traffic had grown lighter, but it still carried a lot of vehicles.

As the driver of one car headed west, he saw a big jet coming in for a landing. At the nation's third-busiest airport, drivers were used to seeing planes passing right overhead, but something did not seem quite right about this approach. The motorist realized that the plane was flying extremely low, even for an aircraft about to touch down. Suddenly the belly of the jet slammed down on the highway, crushing the Toyota right in front of him.

The twenty-year-old driving the Toyota, a young man looking forward to his birthday celebration that night, was decapitated by the plane's Number 1 engine.

The airliner kept going, but the impact with the automobile had killed any hope for a safe landing. Clearing the roadway with its left wing dipping perilously low, the jet sliced through two light poles. Then the wing jammed into the earth. Milliseconds before his death, one of the two pilots yelled his final words: "Oh, shit."

When the wing hit the ground, Meier instinctively ducked, putting his hands on his knees and locking them for support against the crash that he knew would follow.

"God, don't let me die," he prayed. "Let me live."

Still traveling at a ground speed of 220 knots, the jet crashed into one of two 50,000-gallon water tanks near the airport's eastern freight area and exploded into flames. The devastating impact broke the rear quarter of the plane from the rest of the fuselage. With its occupants still alive, that part of the plane shot away like a giant escape pod. The tail section came to a halt lying on its left side.

Still buckled to his seat, Meier hung in the air. He was alive, but he did not know for how long. Watching flight attendant Robinson unstrap herself and climb down a row of seats, Meier quickly did the same thing, using the seats likes steps on a ladder. Reaching the last seat, Meier looked down and realized that he still was about 15 feet in the air. He had no other choice but to let go and fall to the ground.

He hit hard, but it did not hurt him.

In the first few moments after Meier got out of what was left of the airplane, he heard nothing. No crying, no screams. Then the thunderstorm let loose with more rain and winds blowing nearly at hurricane strength. Only seconds went by, but to Meier and the other stunned survivors, it seemed like a half hour. The sound of sirens jarred the Texas businessman back to real time.

Quickly transformed from survivors to heros, Meier and two other men who had made it out of the tail section ran back to the wreckage to help whoever they could find. Meier saw a woman, bleeding from a nasty cut on her head, moving on all fours from beneath the tail section. Pulling his handkerchief from his pocket, Meier pressed it against her wound. Leaving her, he ran to another passenger with obvious trauma to both legs.

"I got over to this girl," he recalled, "and about that time the hail started coming down—marble sized. I picked up some insulation from the plane, about two by four feet, and held it over her upper body. She was saying, 'It hurts, it hurts.'"

Meier did what he could to protect her from the falling ice. "Hold my hand," she pled. "I don't want to die. Don't let me die." Meier tried to comfort her, but he knew that others needed him, too. He went on to help at least six other injured passengers to the ambulances and fire trucks encircling the wreckage.

"I walked up to this one guy I thought was all right," Meier recalled. "He had a cut on the left side of his face, and his jaw was kind of cut up . . . but his eyes were open and he was still sitting there."

Then Meier understood that the man was dead.

Meier did not stop again until he had walked the equivalent of nearly two football fields from the wreckage. At that point two rescuers finally approached him and asked if he needed help. No, he said, all he needed to know was what time it was. He did not intend to miss his flight back to Temple.

Federal aviation investigators later determined that the jet's tail section ripped off at a diagonal, with more seats remaining intact on the right side of the section—where Meier had been—than on the left. Almost everyone in rear of the plane survived. Those on the front side of the seat 34J-to-44C line died. Of the 163 people who had been aboard the flight, only 29 survived. All but two of the survivors had injuries ranging from minor to serious.

The National Transportation Safety Board's investigation revealed that the plane crashed because of wind shear and the pilot's decision—contrary to his company's weather avoidance policy—to continue his approach in obviously bad weather. The agency's report also noted that there was "a lack of specific guidance and training for avoiding/escaping low altitude wind shear."

Wind shear is a sudden change in the direction and speed of wind. Readings from the flight data recorder indicated that the jet encountered a microburst—a powerful downdraft from a thunderstorm—at sixteen seconds past 6:05 P.M. In the following thirty-two seconds, the plane went through three vortexes that were, in effect, horizontal tornadoes. Thirteen seconds after encountering the final vortex, the plane crashed. Investigators later determined that the exact time was 6:08:01 P.M.

The lessons of Flight 191 did not go unheeded. The Federal Aviation Administration now requires all commercial pilots to undergo flight simulator training in coping with wind shear. The computer simulation model is based on the final seconds of Flight 191. Also, since 1993 commercial airliners have been equipped with a system designed to detect wind shear conditions. Finally, by 1998 forty-seven major airports across the nation had been equipped with an improved radar system designed to detect wind shear.

Nationally, no commercial airliner crashes attributable to wind shear have occurred since 1994.

Afterword:
Hurricanes Katrina and Rita

In the summer and early fall of 2005, two powerful hurricanes—Katrina and Rita—had an enormous impact on Texas.

Katrina came ashore near New Orleans on August 29, but it resulted in a migration of humanity unprecedented in modern history. Texas took in some 400,000 evacuees, tens of thousands of them opting to make a new home in the Lone Star state rather than return to Louisiana.

Then, as Texas continued to assist those who had sought shelter from Katrina and the devastation it wrought, an even larger hurricane churned into the Gulf of Mexico, seemingly headed straight to the densely populated Houston-Galveston area.

With a peak wind gust of 235 mph, Rita had grown into a catastrophic Category 5 storm. That made it the fourth most powerful Atlantic storm ever, fueled by the third-lowest barometric pressure ever recorded

"Rita is the strongest storm that I've ever been in," hurricane hunter and Weather Channel meteorologist Lt. Col. Warren Madden said on September 21.

With Rita bearing down on the Texas coast, in the predawn of September 22, the State Operations Center in Austin told the Texas Department of Transportation to do something no one ever thought would be necessary: Convert major segments of Interstates 10 and 45 into one-way thoroughfares outbound from the Houston area.

Having so recently seen television images of hundreds of people stranded on rooftops in flooded portions of New

The Vidor Church of Christ lost its roof after its stained-glass window was blown in by Hurricane Rita.   PHOTO BY BOB MCMILLAN/FEMA

Orleans, more Texans than actually needed to leave undertook an exodus unprecedented in the United States. Multilane freeways slowed to a virtual standstill. Soon people began running out of fuel in the mostly-stop-and-seldom-go traffic jam. Compounding the problem, service stations sold out of gas. Vehicles overheated and stalled in the gridlock, their occupants suffering from the record-breaking heat and humidity.

The enormity of the evacuation was staggering. Later research showed the evacuation had been the largest in world history—an estimated 2.8 million people departed Southeast Texas in sixty hours. In comparison, 2 million fled with the cession of East Prussia to the Soviet Union in 1945, and the Three Mile Island nuclear power plant crisis resulted in the evacuation of 200,000.

Though indirectly, Hurricane Rita claimed its first victims in the early morning hours of September 23 when a chartered bus carrying forty-five nursing home patients evacuated from Bellaire exploded into flames on I–45 in Dallas County. Twenty-three elderly people died in the fire, which investigators later determined started in the vehicle's brake system. Another thirty-seven people died during the evacuation, many from heat exhaustion.

With Houston virtually a ghost town, Rita swung to the northeast and began to lose some of its strength as it hit cooler water. The hurricane finally made landfall at 2:30 A.M. on September 24 near Beaumont as a Category 3 storm with sustained winds of 120 mph, gusting to 155 mph.

Though not the wind and water monster it had once been, the hurricane hit the Beaumont, Orange, and Port Arthur area hard. Many trailers, mobile homes, apartments, and houses suffered heavy damage.

In its final situation report on Rita, issued on December 20, 2005, Texas's State Operations Center listed 11,273 single-family residences as destroyed, along with 9,577 mobile homes and 483 apartments. An additional 23,648 homes, 7,604 mobile homes, and 3,969 apartments sustained major damage from the hurricane.

In monetary terms, insurance losses in Southeast Texas were estimated at some $5 billion. Other sources placed the damage at $9 billion. The total damage estimate came to $16 billion.

Twenty-four Texas counties received presidential disaster declarations, making their residents eligible for federal assistance. But as the Fort Worth *Star-Telegram* reported in a wrap-up story three months after the hurricane, "Not everything will

"Lost Children" room at the Houston Astrodome. Approximately 18,000 hurricane Katrina survivors were housed in the Red Cross shelter at the Astrodome and Reliant center.   FEMA PHOTO/ANDREA BOOHER

be reimbursed, and officials loosely predict it could take three to five years for the economy [of Southeast Texas] to recover."

Rita also destroyed 533 million cubic feet of timber that would have been worth an estimated $3.7 billion in commercial products.

While the state summary listed no casualties, Texas's largest newspaper, the Houston *Chronicle,* tallied 141 deaths linked to the storm or its immediate aftermath. Of those, only six fatalities were attributed directly to the hurricane. Nine people in areas with no electricity available died from carbon monoxide poisoning from improper use of portable generators. The rest, including the twenty-three people killed in the bus crash, had been evacuees.

On February 20, 2006, a task force appointed by Governor Rick Perry released a report making twenty-one recommendations on how Texas could better handle the next major hurricane. The suggestions ranged from the governor needing authority to order multi-jurisdictional evacuations to a recommendation that a plan be developed for sheltering pets during an evacuation.

As spring arrived, state disaster officials organized a preparedness drill to better prepare Texas for the next time.

Appendix:
Other Major Texas Disasters

Excluding criminal mass-casualty incidents, acts of war or terrorism, and events already covered in the book

September 4, 1766

A hurricane heavily damages a Spanish presidio-mission complex known as El Orcoquisac on the east bank of the Trinity River, in what is now Chambers County. No account of fatalities is known, but with a reported 7-foot storm surge, a high percentage of the residents likely perished. The National Weather Service includes the storm in a listing of tropical cyclones believed to have killed twenty-five or more persons. The Spanish abandoned the site four years later.

September 12, 1818

A powerful hurricane strikes Galveston Island. Fierce winds blow and a 4-foot storm surge heavily damages the base of noted pirate Jean Lafitte. The storm destroys four of Lafitte's ships and collapses a fortification known as the Red House. Only six structures on the island remain after the storm sweeps through. One account says that the hurricane resulted in numerous drownings as well as deaths associated with the fall of a cannon when the Red House collapsed. The National Weather Service includes the storm in a listing of tropical cyclones believed to have killed twenty-five or more persons, though no listing of victims is known.

September 25, 1843

Laden with cotton and carrying thirty-one passengers and crew, the steamer *Sarah Barnes* springs a serious leak on her voyage from Galveston to New Orleans. The ship's pumps cannot keep up with the rising water. Deciding to beach the steamer, the captain orders full speed toward the Sabine River. But when the water douses her boiler, the ship begins sinking. She goes down in about 6 fathoms, 40 miles off Sabine Pass. The captain places eighteen people on rafts fashioned from cotton bales and a dozen others in lifeboats. Nevertheless, seventeen people drown, including the master and owner.

August 6, 1844
A hurricane comes ashore near Brazos Santiago, at the mouth of the Rio Grande, killing seventy.

September 7, 1846
Carrying thirty passengers and a crew of twenty-three, the steamship *New York* leaves Galveston on September 5, bound for New Orleans. Only 50 miles out, the ship sails straight into a hurricane. After being badly battered by the storm, the ship sinks in 10 fathoms of water in the predawn hours of September 7. Seventeen passengers and crew members drown.

1848
A cholera epidemic ravages Texas, killing hundreds.

March 26, 1853
A rivalry between captains leads to a race between the steamboats *Farmer* and *Neptune* on their regular run from Houston to Galveston. Twelve miles north of Galveston, the *Farmer*'s boiler explodes. The *Neptune* heaves to and tries to rescue the passengers and crew of its stricken former competitor. Of sixty people onboard the *Farmer,* thirty-six die, including the captain and a dozen members of his crew.

August 8, 1856

The steamboat *Nautilus,* headed to New Orleans from Galveston, sinks in a gale near Galveston on the night of her departure. Of at least thirty people onboard, only one man survives. Also lost are one hundred head of horses, fifty head of cattle, a load of cotton, and a reported $30,000 to $40,000 in gold.

May 31, 1857

Bound for Galveston from Indianola, the steamship *Louisiana* catches fire and sinks in 10 fathoms of water 5 miles offshore from Galveston. Thirty-five passengers and crew lose their lives. The vessel, which carried furniture and lumber, burned to her waterline.

February 12, 1869

On her regular run between New Orleans and the Cypress Bayou port of Jefferson in East Texas, the riverboat *Mittie Stephens* catches fire on Caddo Lake. Sixty-one of the 107 passengers and crew perish when the vessel burns to the waterline. The wreckage of the vessel is located on the Texas–Louisiana state line.

February 14, 1873

The steamboat *Henry A. Jones,* bound from Houston to Galveston with 442 bales of cotton and towing a barge loaded with cut wood, catches fire and goes down 3 miles from Red Fish bar in Galveston Bay. Twenty-nine bodies wash ashore at Edward's Point.

September 16, 1875

City of Waco, a Mallory Line steamship, burns and sinks in a storm off Galveston. All fifty-five people aboard are lost.

December 1885 and January 1886

A series of blizzards sweep across the sparsely settled Panhandle, causing an economic disaster that becomes known as the Big Die-Up. Tens of thousands of free-range cattle drift south to escape the snow, only to reach a barbed-wire fence—built three years earlier by the Panhandle Stock Raisers Association—that crosses most of the Panhandle. Huddled against the fence in the howling wind, thousands of cattle freeze to death or smother. Others are killed by wolves and coyotes. In some counties herd loss is estimated as high as 75 percent. Even wild antelope die in the subzero temperatures. At least five people freeze to death in the worst blizzard, a storm that strikes the Panhandle on January 6, 1886. Livestock losses are estimated at 150,000 to 200,000 head.

October 12, 1886

A hurricane storm surge devastates the community of Sabine (in Jefferson County) and everything for 20 miles inland. One hundred and fifty people drown.

May 15, 1896

A tornado outbreak kills seventy-six people in Cooke, Denton, and Grayson Counties in North Texas. Most of the fatalities occur in Sherman, the Grayson County seat.

February 1899

A mass of arctic air results in an economic disaster, with an estimated 40,000 cattle across the state dying of exposure. Galveston Bay ices over.

June 27–July 1, 1899

A Brazos River flood kills up to thirty-five people and leaves $9 million in damage.

April 5–8, 1900

Torrential rains send the Colorado River on a rampage. Just above Austin, the Lake McDonald Dam washes out, sending a wall of water through a portion of the capital city. The flood claims twenty-three lives and leaves behind $1.2 million in damage.

July 23, 1905

Lightning hits a wood-covered earthen oil storage tank at Humble (Harris County), sparking a fire that spreads to other tanks over a 23-acre area. Fatality estimates range from five to forty men with some 160 mules and horses also killed in the blaze. The intensity of the blaze virtually incinerated all bodies, making an official determination impossible.

April 26, 1906

A tornado in Clay County (in North Texas) kills seventeen people and injures twenty.

May 30, 1909

A tornado strikes the West Central Texas community of Zephyr in Brown County, killing thirty-four people and injuring seventy. The F4 tornado damages fifty homes, six businesses, two churches, and the town high school.

July 21–22, 1909

Velasco takes the brunt of a midsummer hurricane. Forty-one people die, and property damage reportedly tops $2 million.

February 21, 1912

A fire begins in a vacant rail-yard saloon that hoboes use for shelter. The fire spreads quickly, destroying fifty-six blocks in the Houston Heights and Fifth Ward area on the north side of Houston. A church, a school, eight stores, thirteen manufacturing plants, and more than one hundred homes are destroyed. Hundreds are left homeless in the Bayou City's largest fire.

December 1–5, 1913

A rainstorm sends the Brazos River on a rampage. Flooding over a large area of Central and North Texas kills 177 people and causes $8.5 million in property loss.

April 22, 1915

Thirty-five people die in a Colorado River flood, with much of the death and damage in Austin.

August 16–19, 1915

Galveston again is hit by a powerful hurricane. The storm kills 275 and results in more than $56 million in property damage. Devastation would be even worse but for the seawall built to safeguard the city after the 1900 hurricane.

March 5, 1916

El Paso County Jail officials order prisoners to bathe in gasoline, believing that it will protect the group from a typhus outbreak. When a prisoner known as "Hop Head" strikes a smuggled match to light a cigarette, the lockup explodes in flames. Twenty-seven prisoners burn to death and ten more die of severe burns a short time later—the deadliest blaze in El Paso history.

August 18–19, 1916

A hurricane sweeps Corpus Christi, claiming twenty lives and causing $1.6 million in property damage.

January 14, 1918
The derailment of a Houston & Texas Central Railroad passenger train at Hammond (in Robertson County) kills seventeen passengers and injures ten people.

October–November 1918
The "Spanish flu" pandemic kills an estimated 20 million people worldwide—half a million in the United States and several thousand in Texas. Six hundred die in El Paso, where the disease breaks out first among soldiers at Fort Bliss.

August 9, 1919
Tornadoes in Camp, Fannin, Henderson, Red River, Van Zandt, and Wood Counties kill 62 people, injure 195 people, and leave behind $575,000 in damage.

September 14, 1919
A hurricane strikes south of Corpus Christi, with 110-mph winds pushing a storm surge of 16 feet. The unnamed storm takes 284 lives.

December 13, 1922
A Houston East & West Texas Railway (Southern Pacific Lines) passenger train and a light engine collide at Humble, outside Houston. The crash kills twenty-two people and injures eleven.

May 8, 1923
A new oil well explodes in Navarro County in North Texas, fatally burning thirteen people. Two burn victims die later, for a total of fifteen deaths.

May 14, 1923

A tornado cutting through Howard and Mitchell Counties in West Texas kills twenty-three people and injures one hundred.

May 9, 1927

A tornado outbreak kills 28 people and injures more than 200 in Collin, Hunt, and Lamar Counties (Northeast Texas).

May 6, 1930

Tornadoes in Hill, Ellis, and Navarro Counties (North-Central Texas) leave forty-one people dead and $2.1 million in property damage. The same day, tornadoes kill thirty-six more people in DeWitt and Karnes Counties (South Texas) and cause $127,000 in property loss.

1930s

For most of the decade, the Panhandle and West Texas suffer a devastating drought, a situation aggravated by a glutted wheat market. When farmers quit planting, much of the nation's Great Plains region is left unprotected from wind erosion. By the middle of the decade, an area that comes to be called the Dust Bowl covers one hundred million acres over a five-state area. Winds trigger dust storms that turn day into night, with fine dirt drifting like black snow as high as rooftops in some areas. What begins as an ecological disaster becomes an economic one. More than three-and-a-half million people relocate, the genesis of John Steinbeck's classic novel *The Grapes of Wrath*.

Deaths attributable to the Dust Bowl disaster probably were asthma related or suicides. No definitive death toll exists, but the protracted drought killed the spirit of hundreds of thousands farmers and ranchers.

August 13–14, 1932

A hurricane hits the old port of Velasco and the Freeport area, killing forty people and destroying $7.5 million in property.

September 4–5, 1933

A hurricane slams into Brownsville, killing forty people and leaving $16.9 million in damage in its path.

July 25, 1934

The small community of Seadrift is devastated by a hurricane that kills nineteen people and destroys $4.5 million in property.

March 14, 1940

At 8:06 A.M. on U.S. Highway 83 in the Hidalgo County community of Alamo, a truck loaded with Mexican farm workers attempts to cross in front of an approaching Gulf Coast Lines passenger train. The train strikes the truck at 45 mph, killing twenty-nine people and injuring fifteen. This is the deadliest traffic crash in Texas history to date.

July 27, 1943

A "surprise" hurricane—not publicized by forecasters for wartime security reasons—kills nineteen people in the Galveston area and leaves $16.6 million in damage.

January 4, 1946

A freak winter tornado outbreak in East Texas kills twenty-eight people in Anderson, Angelina, and Nacogdoches Counties. Three hundred and ten people suffer injuries in the unusual storm, with property damage estimated at more than $2.5 million.

Wreckage in Higgins following the 1947 Panhandle tornado.
FROM THE AUTHOR'S COLLECTION

April 9, 1947

A tornado outbreak in the Panhandle kills sixty-eight people, injures 272, and causes $1.5 million in damage. An F5 tornado first touches down near White Deer; it stays on the ground until it reaches St. Leo, Kansas, five hours and twenty minutes later. The town of Glazier is destroyed, along with most of Higgins.

August 5, 1947

A truck loaded with construction workers on their way to a job in Dallas collides with a gasoline transport truck 4 miles north of Waxahachie (Ellis County) on U.S. Highway 81. The tank truck explodes moments after the 6:15 A.M. collision, which leaves nineteen people dead. The gasoline truck continues to burn for six hours.

August 4, 1952

At 4 A.M. in light traffic and good weather, two Greyhound Lines buses traveling in opposite directions on US 81 crash head-on 7 miles south of Waco (McLennan County). Both the north- and southbound buses burst into flames. Twenty-eight people, including both drivers, die in the worst commercial bus disaster in American history.

March 13, 1953

Tornadoes in Haskell and Knox Counties kill seventeen people and injure twenty-five.

July 29, 1956

Nineteen men, mostly volunteer firefighters, die trying to douse a blaze at the Shamrock Oil and Gas Corp.'s McKee Plant Tank Farm, near Dumas. Thirty-nine others suffer injuries.

September 1956

A seven-year drought reaches its peak, with all the state's 254 counties experiencing severe drought conditions. The small community of Wink, near Odessa in West Texas, records only 1.76 inches of rain for the year. The drought began moderately in 1949, but by 1951, average precipitation in the state had dropped 40 percent. By 1953 the drought griped three-fourths of the state. This agricultural disaster, which caused enormous economic losses, is still considered the drought of record for Texas.

April–May 1957

The worst drought in Texas history breaks, with two months of torrential rainfall. Flooding claims twenty-two lives across the state.

May 15, 1957

Twenty-one people die when a tornado roars through Silverton in Briscoe County. Eighty people suffer injuries, and property damage is estimated at $500,000.

September 29, 1959

A Braniff Airlines turboprop on its way from Houston to Dallas crashes near Buffalo, killing all thirty-four passengers and crew members. The Civil Aeronautics Board later rules that the Lockheed L-188A Electra crashed after losing its left wing, which wobbled severely due to misalignment of one of the props. The Airline Pilot's Association challenges that finding, listing the cause of the disaster as "unknown" on its records.

September 11–13, 1961

Hurricane Carla zeroes in on tiny Port O'Connor in Matagorda County, but its powerful right hand punches the Galveston-Houston area hard. Thirty-four people die in the giant storm, which produces 175-mph winds and a surge tide of 18.5 feet. Property damage amounts to $300 million.

April 22–29, 1966

Nearly 2 feet of rain triggers flash flooding in the Northeast Texas counties of Gregg, Harrison, Marion, Morris, Smith, Upshur, and Wood. Nineteen people drown. Damage is estimated at $12 million.

May 3, 1968

Braniff Airlines Flight 352 breaks up in turbulence associated with a severe thunderstorm twenty-five minutes after departing Houston for Dallas. The Lockheed L-188A turboprop crashes at 4:48 P.M. near Dawson in Navarro County, killing all eighty-five passengers and crew members. The crash site is only 49 miles from the location of the 1959 Braniff crash.

April 18, 1970

A tornado in Donley County (in the Texas Panhandle) kills seventeen people and injures forty-two. Property damage amounts to $2.1 million.

May 11, 1970

An F5 tornado strikes Lubbock, killing twenty-six people. The damage, estimated at $840 million, places the disaster in the top-five list of costliest U.S. tornadoes.

February 1, 1972

With a crew of thirty-nine people, the tanker *V.A. Fogg* departs from Freeport, having disgorged her cargo of benzene. The captain plans to steam 50 miles into the Gulf of Mexico, anchor, clean his ship's tanks of residue, and then make for Houston to take on another load. But 38 miles off the Texas coast, the ship explodes and sinks. The Coast Guard recovers only three bodies.

May 11–12, 1972

Eighteen people drown in flash floods in Comal and Guadalupe Counties (Central Texas). Property damage is estimated at $17.5 million.

April 29, 1975

A trailer truck loaded with butane overturns in Eagle Pass and explodes into flames, killing the driver and fifteen others who happen to be in the vicinity. Half of the flaming truck flies into a nearby used-car lot, repair shop, and junk yard. Forty cars in the lot are destroyed. The other half of the truck also becomes airborne, landing 400 yards away in a mobile-home park. Realizing that they have no time to stop, people jump from moving cars on Highway 57 to avoid driving into the blazing inferno that spans both sides of the busy roadway.

August 1– 4, 1978

Tropical Storm Amelia rains itself out over Central and West-Central Texas, triggering flash floods in Bandera, Gillespie, Kendall, and Kerr Counties. Twenty-seven people drown, and property damage reaches $50 million. Floods kill another six people in Shackelford County, which receives up to 30 inches of rain.

August 18, 1983

Hurricane Alicia kills twenty-one people in the Galveston-Houston area. Property damage is estimated at $3 billion.

May 22, 1987

A multiple-vortex tornado strikes Saragosa, in Reeves County in far West Texas, at 8:15 P.M. Of the town's 183 residents, 30 die and 121 suffer injuries. The storm destroys 85 percent of the structures in the small community, causing $1.3 million in damage.

August 31, 1988

Bound for Salt Lake City with 102 passengers and six crew members, Delta Flight 1141 crashes on takeoff at Dallas–Fort Worth International Airport. Fourteen people die in the crash, which a National Transportation Safety Board investigation attributes to the flight crew's failure to properly configure the jet's wing flaps and slats.

September 21, 1989

At 7:34 A.M. the driver of a tractor-semitrailer runs a stop sign and crashes into a Mission Consolidated Independent School District bus carrying eighty-one children. The accident occurs on Bryan Road in Alton, a small community in Hidalgo County. The impact plunges the bus into a water-filled gravel pit, where it comes to rest 10 feet underwater. Twenty-one students drown, while another forty-nine vehicle occupants— including the bus driver and the truck driver—suffer injuries in the crash.

October 23, 1989

Multiple explosions and a ferocious fire at the Phillips Petroleum Co. plastics plant in Pasadena kill twenty-two people and injure more than eighty.

September 11, 1991

Continental Express Flight 2574, traveling from Houston to Laredo, spirals to the earth near Eagle Lake, killing all fourteen people aboard. A National Transportation Safety Board investigation reveals that the Embraer 120RT Brasilia turboprop had been improperly maintained, causing its left horizontal stabilizer to fail.

October 15–19, 1994

Nearly 30 inches of rain cause flash flooding in Southeast Texas and claim seventeen lives. Twenty-six counties, including the highly populated Harris County, are declared disaster areas. Property loss is estimated at $700 million.

May 28, 1995

A giant thunderstorm hits the Dallas–Fort Worth metroplex, killing 20 people and injuring 109. Winds up to 70 mph and large hail cause more than $2 billion in damage. The National Weather Service labels the storm the costliest thunderstorm in U.S. history.

May 27, 1997

A tornado strikes Jarrell in Central Texas, killing twenty-seven people. The F5 storm has winds of at least 261 mph.

October 17–19, 1998

Flooding over the Edwards Plateau and along the Texas-Mexico border claims twenty-five lives and leaves behind $500 million in damage.

August 1999

A heat wave over North Texas kills sixteen people in the Dallas–Fort Worth area. The DFW Airport records twenty-six straight days of 100-plus degree readings.

July 2000

Another heat wave, this one in the middle of a ten-month drought, claims thirty-four lives in North and Southeast Texas. Much of South Texas receives a presidential disaster declaration, with the U.S. Department of Agriculture estimating damage from the dry spell at $125 million.

June 5–10, 2001
Tropical Storm Allison comes ashore at Houston, inundating the metropolitan area with up to 40 inches of rain. Flooding kills twenty-two people and causes $5.2 billion in damage, making this the most expensive disaster in Texas history to date.

February 1, 2003
The Space Shuttle Columbia breaks up 38 miles above Northeast Texas on its reentry into Earth's atmosphere, killing its seven crew members, including the first Israeli astronaut. Debris rains down over a wide area of East Texas, western Louisiana, and southern Arkansas, but no one is injured.

September 23, 2005
As Hurricane Rita approaches the Texas coast as a Category 5 storm, a chartered bus loaded with forty-five elderly and special-needs evacuees from a nursing home in the Houston-area city of Bellaire bursts into flames on Interstate 45 in the Dallas County community of Wilmer. Twenty-three of the evacuees die as a result of the early-morning fire, which investigators link to the bus's brake system.

September 24, 2005
Hurricane Rita, weakened to a Category 3 hurricane, strikes Texas at Sabine Pass, east of Beaumont, with 120-mph winds at 2:30 A.M. Counting the twenty-three evacuee deaths described above, the storm takes 141 lives and results in an estimated $16 billion in damage, the state's costliest disaster.

March 11, 2006

A wind-whipped wildfire claims eleven lives, results in the death of an estimated 10,000 head of cattle, and blackens 850,000 acres across the eastern Panhandle. The Texas Forest Service, which coordinated the fire-fighting effort, calls the disaster the worst wildfire in Texas history. It takes firefighters a week to get the blaze fully extinguished.

Bibliography

General Sources

Berman, Bruce D. *Encyclopedia of American Shipwrecks*. Boston: The
　　Mariners Press, 1972.
Boggs, Johnny D. *That Terrible Texas Weather*. Plano: Republic of
　　Texas Press, 2000.
Bomar, George W. *Texas Weather*. Austin: University of Texas Press,
　　1983.
Carr, John T. *Hurricanes Affecting the Texas Gulf Coast*. Austin: Texas
　　Water Development Board, 1967.
Handbook of Texas Online. www.tsha.utexas.edu/handbook/online/.
Interstate Commerce Commission. "Investigations of Railroad
　　Accidents 1911–1966." Online Digital Special Collections,
　　U.S. Department of Transportation. dotlibrary.special
　　collection.net/.
The Lubbock Tornado. Lubbock: Boone Publications, 1970.
Lynch, Dudley. *Tornado: Texas Demon in the Wind*. Waco: Texian
　　Press, 1970.
O'Rear, Mary Jo. "Silver-Lined Storm: The Impact of the 1919 Hur-
　　ricane on the Port of Corpus Christi." *Southwestern Historical
　　Quarterly* CVIII, no. 3 (2005).
Texas Almanac [various editions]. Dallas: *Dallas Morning News*.

"MOST OF US WILL PERISH"
Lost Spanish Fleet (1554)

Allen, Thomas B. "Cuba's Golden Past: Havana's Glittering Era as
　　Spain's New World Port Gleams in Treasures Rescued from the
　　Sea." *National Geographic Magazine*, July 2001.
Arnold, J. Barto III. *Documentary Sources for the Wreck of the New
　　Spain Fleet of 1554*. Translated by David McDonald. Publication
　　No. 8. Austin: Texas Antiquities Committee, 1979.

Arnold, J. Barto III, and Robert S. Weddle. *The Nautical Archeology of Padre Island: The Spanish Shipwrecks of 1554*. New York: Academic Press, 1978.

Perez-Mallaina, Pablo E. *Spain's Men of the Sea: Daily Life on the Indies Fleets in the Sixteenth Century*. Translated by Carla Rahn Phillips. Baltimore: Johns Hopkins University Press, 1998.

Sadler, Jerry. *Treasure Tempest in Texas*. Austin: General Land Office, 1970.

YELLOW JACK CAME TO TEXAS
The Year of Death (1867)

Selected editions of the *Brownsville Daily Ranchero* and *Houston Telegraph and Texas Register*.

Boulware, Narcissa Martin. "Terror in Navasota." *Montgomery County News*, October 8, 2003.

Corpus Christi Advertiser Extra, August 14, 1867. www.library.ci .corpus-christi.tx.us/oldbayview/yellowfeverarticle.htm.

"The Deadly Visitor: Yellow Fever." *Texas Almanac 2004–2005*. Dallas: *Dallas Morning News*, 2004.

Eriksson, Kaye. "Yellow Fever in Galveston." *The Junior Historian*, May 1963.

Givens, Murphy. "The yellow hand of death." *Corpus Christi Caller-Times*, July 15, 1998.

Henley, Susan Rektorik. "Yellow Fever in Texas during the 1800s." *The Czech Voice* 17, no. 2 (2002).

Livingston Linsdsay to Gov. E. M. Pease, October 9, 1867. Records of Elisha Marshall Pease. Archives and Information Services Division, Texas State Library and Archives Commission. www.tsl.state.tx.us/governors/war/pease-lindsay-1.html.

Nixon, Patrick Ireland. *The Medical Story of Early Texas, 1528–1853*. Lancaster, Pa.: The Mollie Bennett Lupe Memorial Fund, 1946.

Smith, Ashbel. *Yellow Fever in Galveston, Republic of Texas, 1839: An Account of the Great Epidemic.* Austin: University of Texas Press, 1951.

The TexGen Web Project. "Grimes County, Texas: 1867 Yellow Fever Victims." www.rootsweb.com/~txgrimes/GrimesYFever.html.

"Yellow Fever in Texas Years Ago," *Austin Statesman,* October 5, 1903.

"THE TOWN IS GONE"
Indianola Hurricanes (1875 and 1886)

Selected editions of the *Cuero Record* and *Victoria Advocate.*

Indianola Scrap Book. Port Lavaca: Calhoun County Historical Survey Committee, 1936, 1974.

Malsch, Brownson. *Indianola: The Mother of Western Texas.* Rev. ed. Austin: State House Press, 1988.

Wolff, Linda. *Indianola and Matagorda Island, 1837–1887.* Austin: Eakin Press, 1999.

"ALL WASHED AWAY"
Ben Ficklin Flood (1882)

Selected editions of the *San Angelo Standard, Tom Green County Times,* and *New York Times.*

Clemens, Gus. *The Concho Country.* San Antonio: Mulberry Avenue Books, 1981.

David Williams to O. Williams, August 27, 1882 and September 10, 1882. Williams Papers, West Texas Collection, Angelo State University.

Elliott, Rev. Morris F. "The Ben Ficklin Flood: Death and Heritage." Paper presented to Edwards Plateau Historical Association, October 2, 1976. West Texas Collection, Angelo State University.

"Karger Tells of Flood Loss at Ben Ficklin." *Frontier Times,* November 1928.

Miles, Susan. "Until the Flood 1867–1882." *Edwards Plateau Historian* 2 (1966).

Spence, Mary Bain. "The Story of Benficklin, First County Seat of Tom Green County, Texas." *West Texas Historical Association Yearbook* 22 (1946).

Tom Green County Historical Preservation League. *Tom Green County: Chronicles of Our Heritage.* Vol. 1, *General History.* Abilene: H. V. Chapman & Sons, 2003.

A CITY IN RUINS
Galveston Hurricane (1900)

Selected editions of the *Galveston Daily News.*

Bixel, Patricia Bellis, and Elizabeth Hayes Turner. *Galveston and the 1900 Storm.* Austin: University of Texas Press, 2000.

Cline, Isaac M. *Storms, Floods and Sunshine.* New Orleans: Pelican Publishing, 1945.

Greene, Casey Edward, and Shelly Henly Kelly, eds. *Through the Night: Voices from the 1900 Galveston Storm.* College Station: Texas A&M Press, 2000.

Larson, Erik. *Isaac's Storm: A Man, a Time and the Deadliest Hurricane in History.* New York: Crown Books, 1999.

Lester, Paul. *The Great Galveston Disaster.* Chicago: Kuhlman, 1900.

Mason, Herbert Molloy. *Death from the Sea.* New York: Dial Press, 1972.

McComb, David G. *Galveston: A History and Guide.* Austin: Texas State Historical Society, 2000.

Stevens, Walter B. "The Story of the Galveston Disaster." Reprint from *Munsey's Magazine,* December 1900.

Weems, John Edward. *A Weekend in September.* New York: Henry Holt, 1957.

Wygant, Alice C. *The 1900 Storm: Galveston, Texas*. Galveston: Galveston County Historical Museum, 1999.

"GOD SEEMED NIGH"
Goliad Tornado (1902)

Selected editions of the *Cuero Record, Houston Post, Victoria Advocate, Houston Chronicle*, and *Goliad Guard*.

Fritz, Karen E. "A Goliad Horror: The Great Tornado of 1902." *South Texas Studies 2001*. Victoria, Tex., Victoria College Press, 2001.

———. "Tornado Victims of the Goliad Tornado of 1902." *Crossroads of South Texas* XXIII, no. 2 (2002).

Goliad County Historical Commission. *The History and Heritage of Goliad County*, Jackie L. Pruett and Everett B. Cole, eds. Austin: Eakin Press, 1983.

THE END OF THE LINE
Locomotive 704 Explosion (1912)

Selected editions of the *San Antonio Express, San Antonio News*, and *San Antonio Light*.

Tucker, Farrell L. "The Great Locomotive Explosion: A Socio-Historical Examination of a Tragedy." colfa.utsa.edu/users/jreynolds/Tucker/exp1.html.

FIRE STRIKES TWICE
Paris Goes Up in Flames (1916)

Selected editions of the *Paris Daily Advocate* and *Paris News*.

Hollis, Herbert Lynn. *Paris Fire of 1916*. Wolfe City, Tex.: Henington Publishing Company, 1982.

Neville, A. W. *The History of Lamar County (Texas)*. Paris: The North Texas Publishing Co., 1937, 1986.

DEADLY DROUGHT-BREAKER
Central Texas Flood (1921)

Selected editions of the *Austin American, Austin Statesman, San Antonio Express, San Antonio News,* and *San Antonio Light.*

Bartlett, C. Terrell. "The Flood of September, 1921, at San Antonio, Texas." Paper no. 1485 presented to the American Society of Civil Engineers, October 5, 1921.

City of Austin. "A Brief History of Austin's Floods." www.ci.austin .tx.us/watershed/floodhistory.htm.

Eckhardt, Gregg. "Flood Control Comes First," subsection of "The San Antonio River." *The Edwards Aquifer Website.* www.edwards aquifer.net/sariver.html.

Ellsworth, C. E. "The Floods in Central Texas in September, 1921." Washington: U.S. Geological Survey Water Supply Paper 488, 1923.

Miller, Char. "Flood of Memories." *Texas Observer,* September 27, 1996.

San Antonio River Improvements Project. "River Improvements Project to Refresh Storied Past of the Historic San Antonio River." www.sanantonioriver.org/history.html.

Scarbrough, Clara Stearns. *Land of Good Water: A Williamson County, Texas, History.* Georgetown: Williamson County Sun Publishers, 1973, 1977.

Taylor, T. D. *All In a Lifetime.* Wolfe City, Tex.: privately published, 1987.

"BLOWN AWAY"
Rocksprings Tornado (1927)

Selected editions of the *Texas Mohair Weekly and Rocksprings Record, San Angelo Standard, San Antonio Express,* and *San Antonio Light.*

Audette, Vicki J., and J. Tom Graham. *Claude H. Gilmer Country Lawyer: Lone Star Lawmaker and Speaker of the House.* Rocksprings, Tex.: privately printed, 2003.

A History of Edwards County. Rocksprings: Rocksprings Woman's Club, 1984.

Jarboe, J. H. "The Rocksprings, Texas, Tornado, April 12, 1927." Washington: *Monthly Weather Review.* April 1927.

Mildred Fleischer Williams, interview with the author, Rocksprings, Texas, June 15, 2004.

Rocksprings Cemetery Family Plots. Rocksprings, Texas.

Sam Thomas, Sonora, Texas, to Mrs. Thomas, correspondence dated April 14, 1927. Author's collection.

THE DAY A GENERATION DIED
New London School Explosion (1937)

Selected editions of the *Dallas Morning News* and *Longview News-Journal.*

American Society of Mechanical Engineers. "An ASME Historic Mechanical Engineering Landmark: Meter-type Gas Odorizer (1937)." www.asme.org/history/roster/H163.html.

Grigg, William N. Jr. "New London School Explosion." www.nlse.org/.

Jackson, Elaine. "East Texas' London Museum." *Texas Magazine,* December 12, 1999.

Jackson, R. L. *Living Lessons from the New London Explosion.* Nashville: Parthenon Press, 1938.

Stowers, Carlton. "The Day a Generation Died." *Scene Magazine,* March 27, 1977.

———. "Today, A Generation Died." *Dallas Observer,* February 21, 2002.

Texas Inspection Bureau. *Report of the High School Explosion and Disaster of London, Texas.* Dallas: 1937.

DEADLIEST FIRE IN TEXAS
Houston's Gulf Hotel Blaze (1943)

Selected editions of the *Houston Chronicle, Houston Post,* and
Houston Press.

Emergency and Disaster Management, Inc. "Hotel Fires."
www.emergency-management.net/hotel_fire.htm.

Houston: A History and Guide. American Guide Series. Houston:
Anson Jones Press, 1942.

McComb, David G. *Houston: The Bayou City.* Austin: University of
Texas Press, 1969.

FUEL TO THE FIRE:
Texas City Explosion (1947)

Behrendt, Ernest. "What Really Happened at Texas City." *Popular
Science* CLXVI (April 1955).

Cross, Farrell and Wilbur Cross. "When the World Blew Up at Texas
City." *Texas Parade,* September 1972.

Cross, Wilbur. "The Charred Memory of Texas City." *Coronet,* April
1957.

Ditzel, Paul. "The Day Texas City Blew Up." *The American Legion
Magazine,* January 1970.

MacKaye, Milton. "Death on the Water Front." *The Saturday Evening
Post,* October 26, 1957.

Minutaglio, Bill. *City on Fire: The Forgotten Disaster that Devastated a
Town and Ignited a Landmark Legal Battle.* New York: Harper-
Collins, 2003.

Olafson, Steve. "The Explosion: 50 Years Later, Texas City Still
Remembers." *Houston Chronicle.* www.chron.com/content/
chronicle/metropolitan/txcity/main.html.

Stephens, Hugh W. *The Texas City Disaster, 1947.* Austin: University
of Texas Press, 1997.

Stone, Ron. *Disaster at Texas City*. Fredericksburg, Tex.: Shearer
    Publishing, 1987.
Texas City Chamber of Commerce. "Texas City, Texas: Its Begin-
    ning, Its Destruction, Its Revitalization." Texas City: 1959.
Wadlington, Cathy. "The Texas City Disaster." *The Texas Historian*
    XXXII, no. 1 (September 1973).
Wheaton, Elizabeth Lee. *Texas City Remembers*. San Antonio: Naylor
    Co., 1948.

"THEY'RE CATCHING HELL"
Waco Tornado (1953)

Fiedler, Randy. "Baylor Faculty, Alums Recall 'Deadliest Tornado In
    Texas History.'" pr.baylor.edu/story.php?id=004288.
Kahan, Archie M. "The First Texas Tornado Warning Conference."
    Southern Regional Headquarters, National Oceanic and Atmos-
    pheric Administration. www.srh.noaa.gov/topics/attach/html/
    ssd97-13.htm.
Moore, Harry Estill. *Tornadoes Over Texas: A Study of Waco and San
    Angelo in Disaster*. Austin: University of Texas Press, 1958.
National Oceanic and Atmospheric Administration. "Historic Tor-
    nado Warning Conference Launched Nation's First Weather
    Radar Network." News Story Archive. www.noaanews.noaa.gov/
    stories/s1163.htm.
"Search for Miss Matkin." *Life* 34, no. 21 (May 25, 1953).
Smith, J. B. "Winds of Change." *Waco Tribune-Herald*, May 11, 2003.
    www.wacotrib.com/hp/content/shared/tx/tornado/story_1.html.
Weems, John Edward. *The Tornado*. College Station: Texas A&M
    University Press, 1977, 1991.

RECORD-SETTING SNOWFALL
Panhandle Blizzard (1956)

Selected editions of the *Amarillo Globe-News* and *Plainview Daily Herald*.

Bomar, George W. *Texas Weather*. Austin: University of Texas Press, 1983.

Larry Todd, interview with the author, Austin, Texas, July 16, 2004.

Mary Kate Tripp, interview with the author, Amarillo, Texas, July 17, 2004.

BUILDING THE BERMUDA TRIANGLE MYTH
SS *Marine Sulphur Queen* Mystery (1963)

Selected editions of the *Austin Statesman, Beaumont Enterprise,* and *New York Times*.

Debbie's Point of View. [Web site dealing with the disappearance of the *Marine Sulphur Queen*] home.pacbell.net/corwind/.

Department of the Navy Naval Historical Center Web site. www.history.navy.mil/faqs/faq8-1.htm.

Gaddis, Vincent. "The Deadly Bermuda Triangle," *Argosy* (February 1964).

In RE Marine Sulphur Queen 460 F.2nd 89 (1972). United States Court of Appeals, Second Circuit.

Rodriguez, Mike. "Dive Report: Fuggedaboudit Wreck, August 19, 2001." www.mikey.net/scuba/dive_reports/fuggedaboudit_01_08_19.html.

United States Coast Guard. *Record of Proceedings of Board of Investigation Inquiring into Losses by Fires and Explosions of the French Steamship Grandcamp and U.S. Steamships Highflyer and Wilson B. Keene at Texas City, Texas, 16 and 17 April, 1947*. Washington, D.C.: September 24, 1947.

United States Coast Guard. "SS *Marine Sulphur Queen:* Disappearance of at Sea on or about 4 February 1963." Washington, D.C.:
Marine Board of Investigation, August 23, 1963.

FLASH FLOOD
Tragedy in Terrell County (1965)

Selected editions of the *San Angelo Standard-Times* and *San Antonio
Express.*
Scogin, Russell Ashton. *The Sanderson Flood of 1965: Crisis in a
Rural Community.* Alpine, Tex.: Sul Ross State University, 1995.

TERRIBLE TUESDAY
Wichita Falls Tornado (1979)

Selected editions of the *Wichita Falls Times Record News.*
Jones, Larry W. "Western Sizzlin' Worker Was Crushed." *Remember-
ing Terrible Tuesday. Wichita Falls Times Record News* Online.
www.trnonline.com/tornado/articles/jones.htm.
Lazenby, Gwen. "Family Lucky To Be Alive after Tornado." *Remem-
bering Terrible Tuesday. Wichita Falls Times Record News* Online.
www.trnonline.com/tornado/articles/lazenby.htm.
Templar, Le. "Winds of Change: Tornado Sparked New Spirit in
City." *Remembering Terrible Tuesday. Wichita Falls Times Record
News* Online. www.trnonline.com/tornado/articles/winds_of_
change.htm.
The Wichita Falls, Vernon & Lawton Tornadoes. Wichita Falls, Tex.:
C. F. Boone, 1979.

"HORIZONTAL TORNADOES"
The Crash of Delta 191 (1985)

Selected editions of the *Dallas Morning News* and *Fort Worth Star-Telegram*.

Chandler, Jerome. *Fire and Rain: A Tragedy in American Aviation.* Austin: Texas Monthly Press, 1986.

Kilroy, Chris. "Special Report: Delta Air Lines Flight 191." www.airdisaster.com/special/special-dl191.shtml.

National Aeronautics and Space Administration. "Technology For Safer Skies." *The Space Educator's Handbook.* vesuvius.jsc.nasa .gov/er/seh/pg56s95.html.

The National Aviation Safety Data Analysis Center, Federal Aviation Administration. "National Aviation Safety Data Analysis Center Brief Report." www.airdisaster.com/reports/ntsb/AAR86-05 .pdf.

About the Author

MIKE COX is the author of a dozen books on Texas history and other subjects. He was the communications manager for the Texas Department of Transportation while Texas absorbed hundreds of thousands of evacuees during Hurricanes Katrina and Rita. Before that, he spent fifteen years with the Texas Department of Public Safety as a public information officer and was a newspaper reporter—all good background for writing about disasters and rescue efforts in Texas.